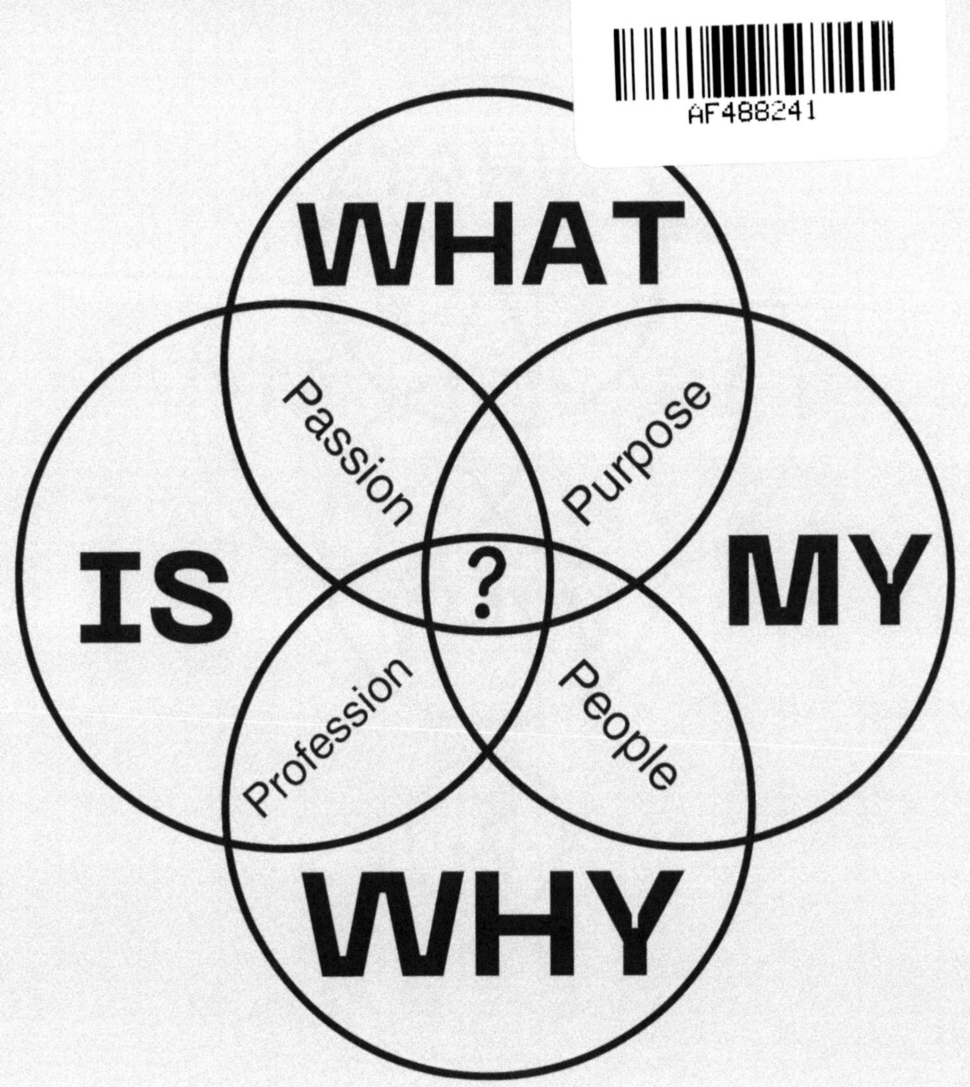


# HOW YOU CAN USE IKIGAI TO CLARIFY YOUR PURPOSE

# BIJAN MACHEN

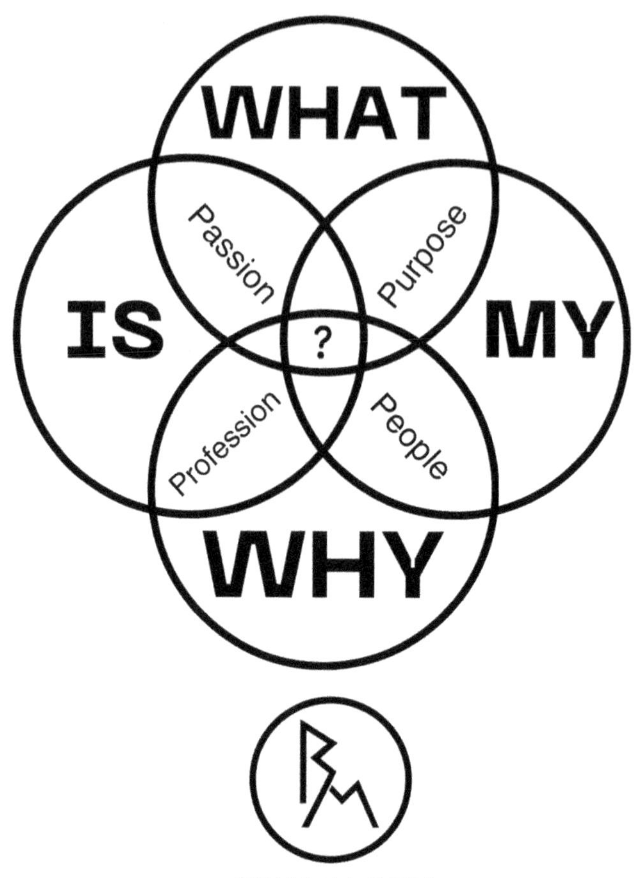



eBOOK + ISBN: 979-8-9896613-8-1
HARDCOVER + ISBN: 979-8-9896613-1-2
AUDIOBOOK + ISBN: 979-8-9896613-7-4
PAPERBACK + ISBN: 979-8-9896613-9-8
Library of Congress Control Number: 2024904264




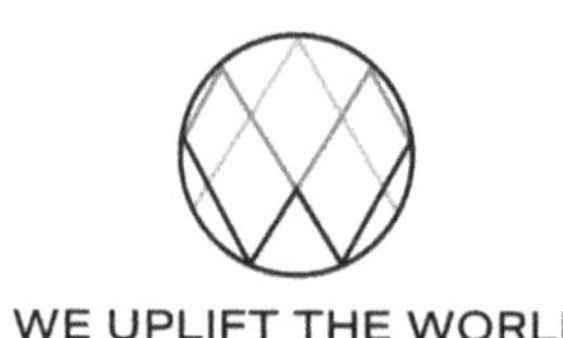

# YOU ARE A WINNER

## Join A Winning Community!

Subscribe and you will be the first to know when I share new art, inspiration, and information to help you win more abundantly.

bijanmachen.com

# ABUNDANCE UNIVERSE PODCAST

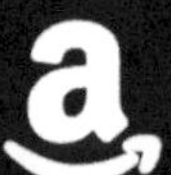
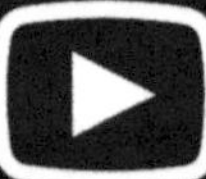

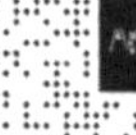

# WHAT IS MY WHY?

Bijan Machen

How You Can Use Ikigai To Clarify Your Purpose

# Table of Contents

This book is a work of transformational art,
dedicated to everyone willing to learn, grow, and
create their best life.

Shine your light. You are a Super Star!

# MY WHY

I felt stuck. You know those days when getting out of bed feels like fighting against gravity? That was my life — lucrative career, outward success, and an echoing sense of "Is this it?" I was drowning in a sea of navy blue monotony, suffocating under expectations that weren't even mine. I was confused, wondering if it was possible to make money doing something I actually loved to do.

Then I discovered ikigai — the idea that true fulfillment comes when you find the sweet spot between what you love, what you're good at, what the world needs, and what you can be paid for. It immediately resonated, and the concept of ikigai became my north star to freedom.

The first step was brutal self-honesty. I'd spent years numbing the voice inside that whispered my forgotten dreams of being an artist. It was terrifying to hear that voice, to admit that my true passions held no place in my neatly structured life. But, like peeling back the vinyl wrap off a Lamborghini, I revealed vibrant hues of who I used to be — the kid who devoured books, the one who'd get lost in a drawing, who practiced orating elaborate motivational speeches to his action figures. What if I pursued my dream of becoming a full-time creative entrepreneur?

# WHAT IF?

That question led to exploration. Small steps at first: lunchtime online workshops, evening art courses on topics of interest. Rekindling a dormant passion, even if it's a bit rusty, is fuel for your soul. The courage to quit my suffocating tech job came later, driven by the same desperation as someone gasping for air. Living a mundane life was unacceptable. I yearned for a life of purpose. I needed to create a lifestyle that I absolutely loved. ASAP!

Initially, I didn't have a grand plan, just the certainty that every day spent in that corporate world was another day stolen from my dreams. I knew I had to change my life!

So, I did just that. I decided to go all in on my dream. I saved up all the money I had and enrolled in ArtCenter College of Design's MFA program. I graduated early, started selling my art, and I founded my own education company, We Uplift The World.

Now, I help other people manifest abundance + awaken to their purpose, reprogram their minds, and craft a beautiful life aligned with who they truly are. I encourage everyone to seek freedom, dream big, and experience all that life has to offer. It can get messy, sometimes even scary, but it's oh so worth it.

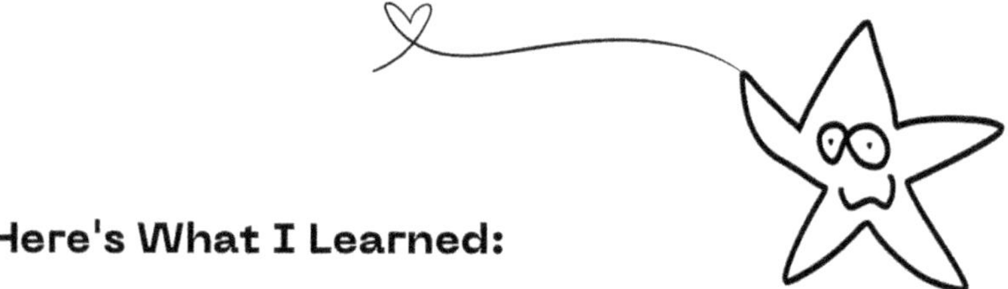

## Here's What I Learned:

You owe it to yourself to try. Quitting my high-paying, stable job was terrifying, but even worse was the thought of never pursuing what made my heart sing. Starting small is key. I began selling my art and sharing my journey locally, which led me to teaching workshops to help others tap into their creative potential. Seeing people rediscover their spark for life…that was priceless.

The truth is, your dreams haven't expired. They're just buried under layers of fear, doubt, and societal programs. Finding your WHY isn't about a dramatic makeover, it's a conscious uncovering of those buried desires. You go as far as you can with what you have now, and as you intentionally move further along on your journey, your vision will deepen, your awareness will expand, and you will live in the flow. When you are in your flow, everything in your experience is aligned. Life becomes easy, and you just know that you're doing what you were born to do. Every human on earth deserves to feel this joy.

# I Want You To Know:

Your WHY isn't going to come knocking with business cards. You're gonna have to do a bit of searching. It starts with curiosity. What did you love as a kid? What can you talk about for hours? What fills you with enthusiasm, even alongside the fear? Lean into that. Find what sets you free.

Try new things! The more you experiment, the clearer your path becomes. You won't find all the answers overnight, but every moment of living authentically fuels your inner compass. Trust me, nothing feels better than living a fun, free, abundant lifestyle that's aligned with your WHY.

You will have to work against fear, doubt, negative programs, and a lot of other forces in order to manifest your best life, but it gets easier along the way, especially when you have effective tools, great relationships, and an abundance mindset. Just keep going. You will win!

The world needs your unique contribution, that thing only you can offer. Stop surviving, and start living life on your own terms. You'll be surprised when you choose to use the strength you didn't know you had.

You are much more than the sum of your mistakes, traumas, and limitations. You are a child of GOD, endowed with the seeds of greatness, and the ability to achieve anything. Believe in yourself. You're awesome!

This book offers a pathway to understanding and accepting the core parts of oneself, to create more wholeness. It's a compilation of questions, tools, guides, planners, and affirmations designed to empower your mindset. I also included images of my abstract art to help expand your imagination. The goal is to help you master your thoughts and create clarity around your life's purpose. I put in the work and did all of the awareness exercises that I'll share with you and now I live the life of my dreams. I am living every day on-purpose and my WHY is to share my knowledge, so that you too can love the life you live!

# FEEL GOOD NOW

Let's talk about your feelings. Feeling good is the master key to success. The way you feel will guide your next steps, leading you to make better feeling decisions, leading you to more success. Trust your natural instincts because your 'gut feeling' is almost always right. If you're not feeling great, choose more positive thoughts, and take actions that make you feel better. Change your physiology, stand up straight, get more sunshine, breathe deep, stretch, and exercise your body. KNOW what makes you feel better. Master your energy.

Your feelings represent the intuitive control center of your emotional guidance system. When you are tuned in properly, emotions act as your personal GPS, directing you to your desired destination. Your intuition will always point you in the best direction. You manifest success by consciously raising your energetic frequency and moving toward the best-feeling vibrations. Drink spring water with fresh lemon juice every morning. Eat clean, high-vibrational foods. You are what you eat. Stay uplifted! The higher your frequency, the easier it is to receive GOD's guidance. Vibrate higher!

The ultimate goal in every moment is to 'feel good now.' Being healthy, responsible, productive, lucrative, and successful feels good to you, so continue doing what you need to do to feel better. Tell yourself "I FEEL GOOD NOW"

**SUN:** The sun is a healer. It literally powers up everything on earth, especially you! Taking a walk outside in the sun will always make you feel better. Breathe in the sun. Exercise in the sun. Read this book in the sun. Get as much sunlight as possible. Shine!

Feeling **ikigai** involves pursuing enjoyable activities with a sense of achievement and awareness while fulfilling your life's purpose. It is future-oriented and goal-seeking.

Feeling **shiawase** is characterized by delight and peace, oriented towards the present moment. It's about being aware of your feelings RIGHT NOW.

The thoughts you think and the words you speak will effect the way you feel. By focusing on feeling better, speaking productive words, and choosing good-feeling activities, you will raise your vibration. Elevated frequencies of vibration contribute to a heightened sense of well-being, enabling you to attract more positive people, places, and experiences into your life. Improve the quality of your thoughts, move your body, and increase the uppage!

The objective is to enhance your emotional state by resonating at a higher frequency. Cultivating peaceful lifestyle habits can facilitate this journey, drawing you nearer to an energetic state of love, joy, and fullness.

Transforming your emotional state is enhanced through prayer, meditation, focused actions, and by engaging in the exercises outlined in this book. The included activities and questions are specifically designed to raise your consciousness and elevate your vibrational frequency. Embrace these practices as pathways to a more enriched and harmonious existence. Let your WHY guide you. Glow up!

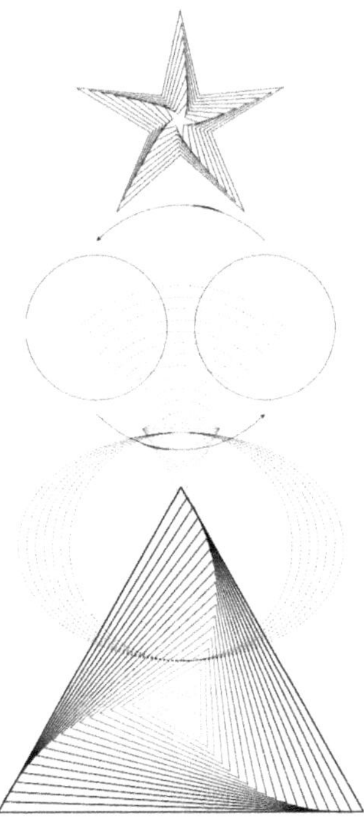

You must master the inner life to be effective in the outer life...

# The Neurochemistry of Feelings

There's a lot of science to feeling good. Our brains produce specific chemicals that profoundly impact our mood and overall well-being. Here's a quick summary:

- **Dopamine** (The Reward Chemical): Motivates us to pursue things that bring pleasure or fulfill needs. We get a 'hit' when achieving goals or enjoying something.
- **Serotonin** (The Mood Stabilizer): Affects mood, appetite, and sleep. Low levels are linked to depression. Natural boosts make us feel content and emotionally stable.
- **Oxytocin** (The Love Hormone): Facilitates bonding, trust, and intimacy. It lowers stress and increases feelings of connectedness with others.
- **Endorphins** (Natural Painkillers): Released in response to physical activity or laughter, endorphins reduce pain by sparking euphoric feelings.

## Emotional Release & Gratitude

- **Emotional Processing:** Allow yourself to feel emotions without suppression. Yell, cry, laugh, and seek safe spaces to express fully. Love yourself more.
- **Forgiveness:** Practice forgiveness for yourself and others. Release resentment and past hurts. Let it go.
- **Gratitude:** Actively acknowledge things you're grateful for. Keep a gratitude journal to cultivate this mindset throughout the day.  You'll feel better by being grateful.
- **EFT Tapping:** Do a YouTube search for "The Callahan Technique" and "Emotional Freedom Technique". This exercise will help you remove energetic blocks, clear your neural pathways, and improve energy flow.

## Energy Work

- **Breath+Work:** Explore techniques like Wim Hof, box breathing, or pranayama (yogic breathing) to shift your energy, clear your mind, and release tension.
- **Yoga:** Combine physical postures (asanas) with focused breathing to increase vibrancy and balance. Stretch daily.
- **Tai Chi:** Practice moving your energy with Tai Chi.

# Physical Well-Being

- **Healthy Diet:** Emphasize organic whole foods, fruits, and vegetables. Limit processed foods and sugar, which lower vibration. Eat more living foods. Eat clean.
- **Hydration:** Drink fresh lemon water to support your body's natural cleansing processes. No more soda.
- **Exercise:** Move your body regularly — walking, dancing, jump rope, stretching, anything that energizes you.
- **Sleep:** Prioritize sufficient, quality sleep every night.

## Prayer, Mindfulness & Meditation

- **Prayer:** Ask GOD for guidance and clarity as you move through your day. Listen to the Holy Spirit and take action on your intuition. Read your Bible, stay aware, and be open to experiencing wonderful miracles.
- **Meditation:** Find a technique that suits you (guided, TM, breathing, etc.) Start with short sessions and gradually increase. Clear your mind daily.
- **Mindfulness:** Engage fully in the present moment without judgment. Mindfulness exercises or simply focusing on your breath can be great. Be still. Breathe.
- **Visualization:** Create mental images of positive outcomes, goals, and a high-vibrational state of being. Picture abundant success in your mind's eye. Feel it.

## Environment & Lifestyle

- **Nature:** Spend more time outdoors. Grounding, sunlight, and fresh air are energetically healing. Nature is a healer.
- **Declutter:** Release items that no longer serve you to unburden both your space and energy. Give stuff away.
- **Uplifting Media:** Be mindful of your consumption. Select positive, inspiring books, movies, and music.
- **Positive Surrounding:** Connect with supportive, high-vibe people who uplift you. Good vibes only!
- **Acts of Service:** Contribute to others. Compassion has a ripple effect and elevates vibrations. Do more good.
- **Consistency:** Integrate good habits every single day!
- **Intuition:** Pay attention to what resonates most with you. Stay in the flow and trust your gut feeling.
- **Patience:** The journey of raising your vibration is ongoing. There is no limit to how high you can elevate your consciousness. Stay up! Everything counts. Be patient with yourself and celebrate your progress along the way!

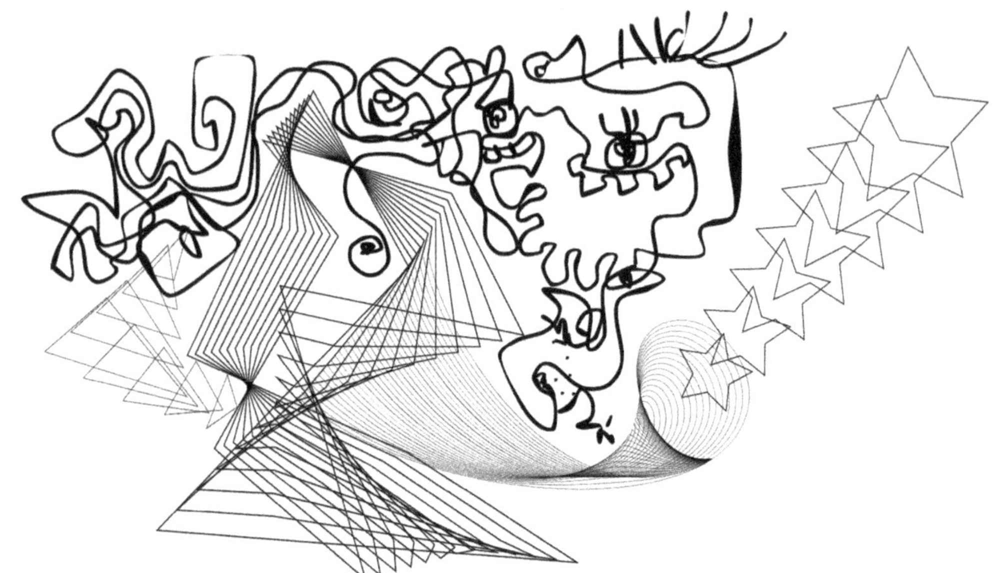

# YOUR WORDS CREATE YOUR REALITY

# SPEAK ONLY OF WHAT YOU WANT TO CREATE

# BELIEVE IN YOUR POWER

# AFFIRM YOUR TRUTH

# LIVE YOUR BEST LIFE NOW!

# WHO ARE YOU?

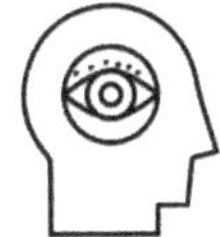

**"Who am I?"**

+ Be yourself. Explore yourself. Express yourself. Love yourself.

**"What do I desire?"**

+ It's important to be specific and intentional with your answer. Knowing what you want to create in every moment will help you prioritize your actions and make decisions that align with your goals. Only consider your true desires, not what other people say you should want. What do YOU want to create? WHY?

**"What am I grateful for?"**

+ Gratitude is a powerful tool for cultivating a positive mindset and increasing your self-awareness. You have abundant blessings in your life right now. Take time daily to reflect on the things in your life that you appreciate and express gratitude for them. By doing so, you will receive more resources to create what you want. The energy of being grateful produces more things to be grateful for. Whenever you want to express extreme gratitude, you can joyfully and enthusiastically say **ABUNDANCE ALERT!**

**"What am I doing to take care of myself?"**

+ Self-care is essential for maintaining physical, emotional, and mental well-being. The way you take care of your body is a direct reflection of your beliefs about yourself. Exercise daily and take time to engage in activities that recharge you. Health is wealth. Prioritize health!

**"What am I doing to create a positive change in the world?"**

+ Your identity is connected to the way you're making a positive impact in the world. Consider how you can use your skills, knowledge, and time to contribute to causes that matter to you. Whether you help people through your business, your job, volunteering, or donating to charity, everything you do while living your ikigai counts towards creating a better world. Remember, one small act of kindness can make a big difference!

# **DESIRE:** What do I Want and WHY?

Before you can achieve personal mastery, you must first decide "What am I mastering?" This way you'll know exactly how to optimize your habits for success.

Delve deep within yourself to uncover what truly ignites your passions and drives you forward. When we ask ourselves, "What do I really want?" we open the door to a world of new possibilities. Our imaginations expand when we ask WHY? Asking WHY allows you to clarify your goals, identify your motivations, and set a clear path toward absolute fulfillment. Trust your intuition. Acquire the skills you need to get where you want to be and go for it!

Our desires are like guiding stars, leading us towards our true purpose and happiness. They are the fuel that propels us to take action, make choices, and pursue our dreams. By exploring the root of our desires, we gain insight into our innermost desires and aspirations, helping us create a life that is truly aligned with our authentic selves. Trust your desires.

The next time you find yourself pondering the question, "What do I really want?" remember that your desires are not random whims. They are powerful forces waiting to be transmuted into real life experiences. Embrace your desires, internalize them, and follow your heart? What do you want?

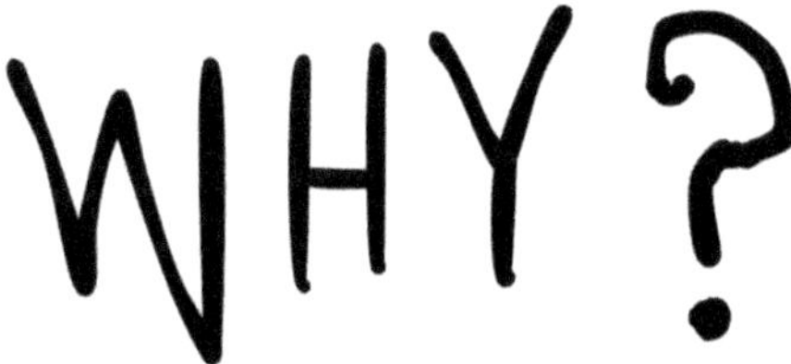


As you navigate these questions, look for patterns in your responses and make micro-adjustments. Your WHY is a tool for discernment. Consider what 'aligns with' or 'deviates from' your ikigai, and discern the elements that contribute most positively to your sense of purpose and fulfillment. Eliminate anything that doesn't move you closer to what you desire.

# 3 <u>KEY</u> QUESTIONS

Ask yourself these 3 key questions as often as possible to create more clarity and self-awareness. You can ask these questions if you ever feel stuck, confused, lost, or unmotivated. I recommend you do this activity every single day. Remind yourself WHY you're here. Review your WHY often and notice your transformation over time.

## WHO AM I?

- _____________________________________________________

_____________________________________________________

_____________________________________________________

_____________________________________________________

## WHAT DO I WANT?

- _____________________________________________________

_____________________________________________________

_____________________________________________________

_____________________________________________________

## WHY?

- _____________________________________________________

_____________________________________________________

_____________________________________________________

_____________________________________________________

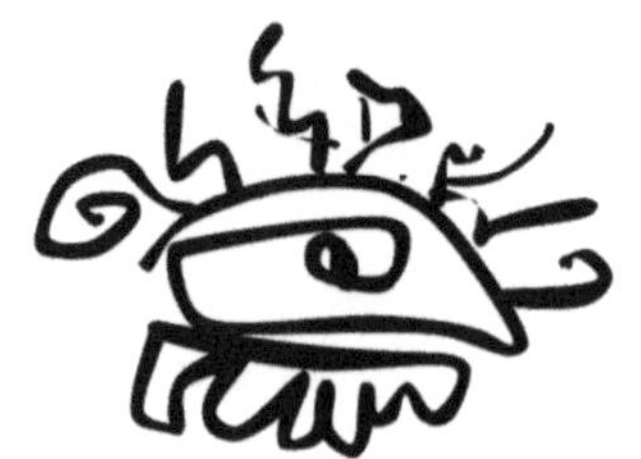

# MAKE YOUR

# DECISION

# &

# GO!

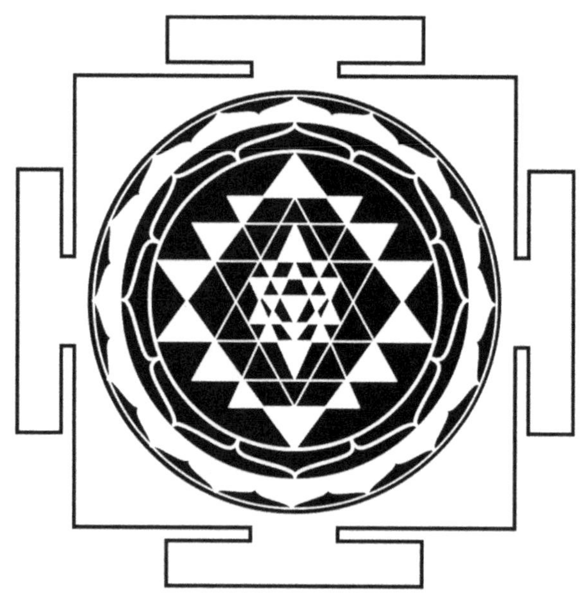

The concept of ikigai encompasses the idea of deciding one's "reason for being." It is a combination of four key elements: what you love, what you are good at, what the world needs, and what you can be paid for. When these four elements intersect, you create a sense of fulfillment, purpose, and meaning in your life. This is your ikigai.

Ikigai has origins in Okinawa, Japan, which is known to have historically high numbers of citizens who live to be over 100 years old (centenarians). The word IKIGAI combines two smaller Japanese words: "iki" (meaning "life") and "gai" or "kai" (meaning "worth" or "value").

Ikigai is not just about finding a job or career that pays well, it's about discovering something that ignites your passion and allows you to contribute to society in the most meaningful way. Ikigai is about creating your harmonious balance and living a life you enjoy, both personally and professionally.

I like to think of ikigai in terms of **The 4 P's**
   1. **Passion**
   2. **Purpose**
   3. **People**
   4. **Profession**

It all begins with YOU. What have YOU always had an affinity for? What do YOU desire to achieve? The pursuit of ikigai requires self-reflection, introspection, and a willingness to explore new opportunities. Becoming the highest version of yourself will demand patience and perseverance, but the rewards are immeasurable. Ikigai provides a blueprint for you to create a life that is not only successful but also fun, fulfilling, aligned, and purposeful. The world needs the best version of YOU.

You can use ikigai to perform an excavation of the soul, unveiling the layers that reveal your purpose. Through guided reflections, contemplative exercises, and profound narratives, you will navigate the terrain of self-discovery, bringing to light the WHY behind your actions and aspirations!

# THE 4 P's

**PASSION:** What do you love?
- What activities never fail to capture your interest?
- When do you experience genuine happiness?
- Recall the last time you lost track of time — what were you doing?
- Reflect on past experiences that left you feeling energized.
- Identify something you would continue doing even without monetary compensation.

**PURPOSE:** What are you good at?
- Identify skills or talents that come naturally to you.
- What do people seek your assistance for?
- What do you excel at effortlessly?
- Consider aspects of your job that you find fun & easy.
- In what areas do you stand out in your social, professional, or community circles?

**PEOPLE:** What does the world need?
- Identify ways you can contribute meaningfully to others.
- Consider societal problems you'd like to address.
- Assess the overall impact of your work. Be prolific!
- Meet more people. Connect and collaborate more often.
- Explore opportunities to increase your involvement in the community. Look for people to help with your key skills.

**PROFESSION:** What will people pay you for?
- What would make you feel more seen and more successful?
- Assess the long-term viability and scalability of your work. How can your WHY help more people in less time?
- What is your most lucrative skill? Double down on that.
- Does the current career vehicle match your destination?
- Choose a means of delivering value and making money that can get you to where you want to be expeditiously.
- If you're already financially successful in your line of work, what would make you feel more fulfilled moving forward? What does the next level look like for you?
- Decide what's most important to you and choose to only work on exciting, important projects. This will make you outstanding, and the best in your niche.
- How do you want to live your days? Visualize your ideal lifestyle, write it down, and create it! This is your legacy.

# What Do You Love?

At the heart of ikigai lies a profound exploration of personal passion. Think about what you've always loved to do. Is there an activity that you engage in where time stops, and you find yourself in the zone? What is your magnificent obsession?

Your "reason for being," is more than just finding a job that pays the bills. It's about discovering something that ignites a fire within you, something that you're passionate about, and eager to pursue with your whole heart.

Live a lifestyle you love by aligning your professional pursuits with genuine affection. When you're completely aligned, work no longer feels like a chore, but rather a fulfilling and purposeful endeavor. The art of loving what you do is not just about finding the "perfect job", it's about creating the perfect blend of your skills, interests, and values.

When you clarify your WHY and integrate it into your daily habits, you tap into a wellspring of energy and motivation that propels you forward and fills your life with joy and meaning. What does that look like for you?

Identifying your passion and aligning it with your actions is a journey that requires deep reflection, introspection, and honesty. It will take time and effort to uncover what truly drives you, but it's a worthwhile pursuit. When you love what you do, you're more likely to experience a sense of fulfillment, even when faced with challenges and setbacks. Work doesn't feel like work when you genuinely love what you're doing. Your passion will fuel your creativity and inspire you to explore new ideas and create new possibilities. Make a promise to yourself to do more of what you love!

When you are in a good feeling flow, doing what you love, it will have a positive impact on your mental and physical well-being. Studies have shown that people who have a strong sense of purpose tend to live longer, healthier lives. That's why Okinawa, Japan, where the concept of ikigai originated, is known to have the most centenarians. By pursuing your ikigai, you're not only enhancing your own life, but you're also contributing to the world in a positive, meaningful way.

Take some time each day to reflect on what you truly love to do. What activity makes you feel more excited, grateful, and energized? What's fun for you? What are you naturally good at? Have you received accolades for any accomplishments in the past? What's the most interesting industry to you? What moves you? What inspires you to be better? What have you always seen yourself being the best at? What is your dream?

Write the answers to these questions in your journal daily. The more you write, the clearer your mind, and your plans will become.  Script your success. Speak to yourself out loud and affirm your truth. This will increase your conviction and strengthen the belief of your vision.

What do you love to do?

----------------------------------------------------------------
----------------------------------------------------------------
----------------------------------------------------------------

WHY?

----------------------------------------------------------------
----------------------------------------------------------------
----------------------------------------------------------------

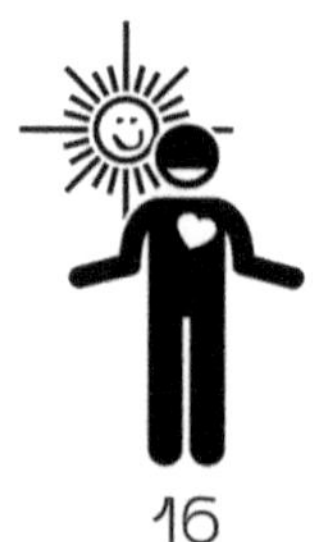

# 2

# What Are You Good At?

The next dimension of ikigai requires you to reflect on your innate skills and talents. Look inward, for this is where your mastery will be honed.

Personal mastery is about understanding your unique abilities and optimizing them to achieve big goals that make a meaningful impact in the world. What are you good at? What do you enjoy doing well? What feels like the thing you were born to do? What will your legacy be? How can your skills be the solution to a challenge that someone in the world is facing right now?

Choose to work in an industry that is aligned with your top skills. This way, if work projects ever get challenging, you will still have a genuine interest in your industry, and you'll find joy in your work because you're good at it. This will give you the flow and flexibility to experiment with different ways of creating success within your niche that bring you more fulfillment, alignment, and increased income.

You can always be improving upon your strengths, but this doesn't mean that you should ignore your weaknesses entirely. Rather, it's about acknowledging shortcomings and finding ways to work around them or turn them into strengths. By making daily micro-improvements, you will create a more well-rounded skill set and become even more valuable to yourself and others. Learn from the masters and become a master.

Maintain a deep appreciation for your GOD-given gifts and commit to continuous improvement. Set a conscious intention to become an expert in your chosen area of focus. Use your talent to make a positive difference in people's personal and professional lives.

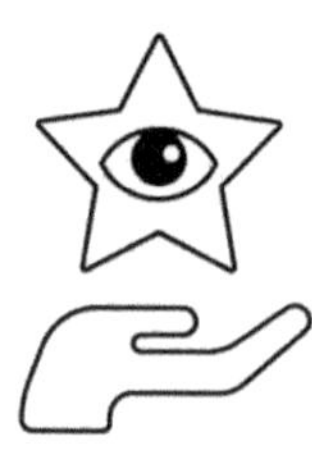

What have people always told you you're good at?

-------------------------------------------------------------

Where do you feel most confident?

-------------------------------------------------------------

What do you want to be the best at?

-------------------------------------------------------------

WHY?

-------------------------------------------------------------

Bring to light your natural talents and strengths that others have recognized. The feedback we receive from others can highlight the unique qualities that make us who we are. Integrate your life by choosing projects, jobs, and business partners who are aligned with your values, your WHY, and your ikigai.

Reflect on your aspirations and dreams for the future. What is the one thing you want to be, more than anything else in the world? WHY? Understanding the reasons behind your desire to become great at something is key to fueling your determination and perseverance. What makes you feel like a Super Star? What is your "Main Thing"? Ikigai will guide you as you integrate personal fulfillment, a sense of accomplishment, and your desire to make a positive impact on the world.

Having a clear WHY will help you stay focused and committed to your goals, especially when faced with challenges and setbacks along the way. Follow what feels good to you. Pray, meditate, and listen to GOD. Always remember, you are a Super Star!

# YOU ARE A CREATOR

## NOT A CRITIC

## NOT A COWARD

## NOT A CONSUMER

# BE A CREATOR

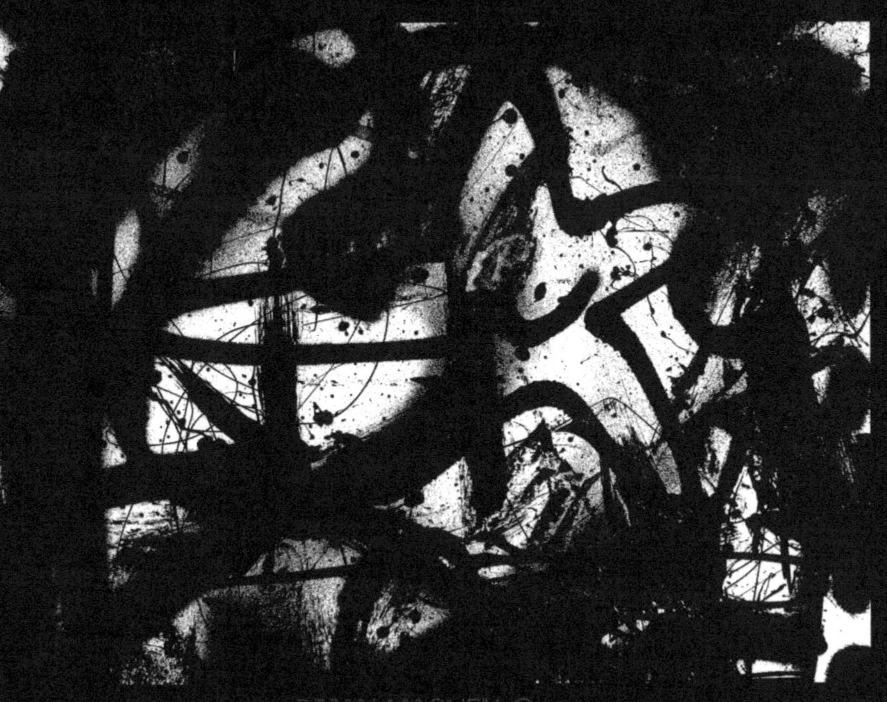

# 3

# What Does The World Need?

Moving beyond personal introspection, the next phase of ikigai calls for a conscientious consideration of societal needs. Here, we analyze the symbiotic relationship between individual aspirations and collective welfare, emphasizing your role as a conduit for productive, positive energy. What is your mission?

As you clarify your life's mission, it's important to consider what the world needs most right now. This way of thinking is deeply rooted in Japanese culture, where giving back to the community is a fundamental value. Many companies in Japan have a strong commitment to corporate social responsibility and prioritize contributing to society as much as generating profits.

What do you care about deeply? There are so many global issues that require our attention, from education and economics to climate change, equality, and social justice. It can be overwhelming to choose just one cause to dedicate your life to, but it's important to remember that every positive action counts toward making your world better. One way to approach your decision is to consider a problem that you believe you are called to solve using your GOD-given gifts and natural talents.

Dream big! The universe is abundant and your aspirations should be so large that they will make a lasting impact on the world. Think about your purpose with the mindset of abundance. The abundance mentality not only benefits society as a whole, but it also enhances your reputation and accelerates your success. You are a genius with the power to create anything you desire!

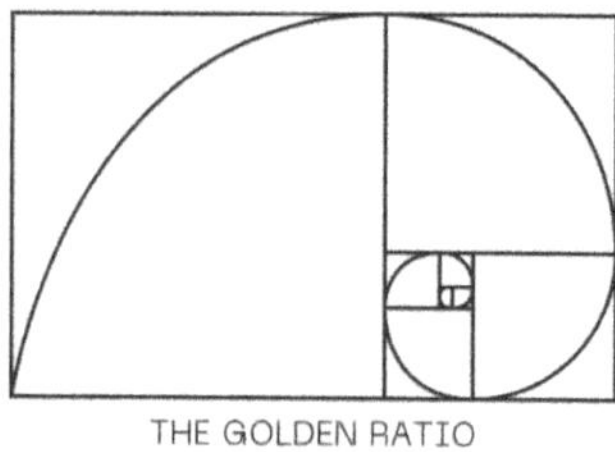

THE GOLDEN RATIO

# Depth of Vision

Think about the long-term effects of your chosen mission. Does what you're doing now contribute to your grand vision? Will your contribution have a positive influence on future generations? How? Will you help create a better world for millions of people, or just a select few?  Visualize. Think deeper. Dream bigger!

Your vision should be so massive that it feels almost impossible to accomplish in one lifetime. That means your vision is deep, and the mass of your thoughts will create a magnetic gravitational pull in the universe, attracting everything and everyone you'll need to manifest the desires of your heart. Trust GOD and believe in your vision. You can be, do, & have anything you want. Just focus on one thing at a time.

What do you believe the world needs right now?

------------------------------------------------------------

How will you use your ikigai to uplift people?

------------------------------------------------------------

WHY?

------------------------------------------------------------

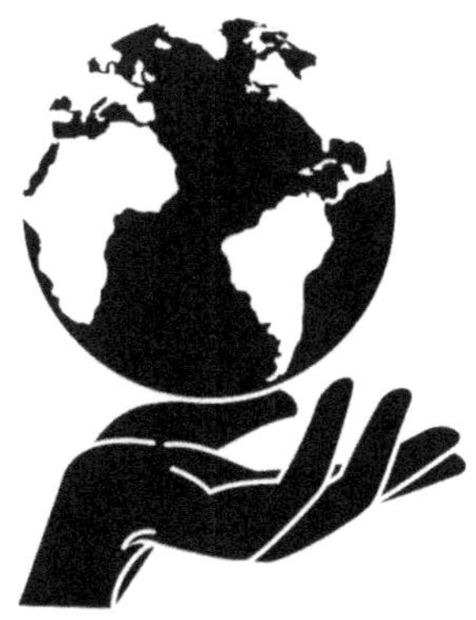

# WE UPLIFT THE WORLD

# 4

# What Will People Pay You For?

Money is an abundant renewable resource that comes to you after you provide value to other people. Money gives us more freedom, more options, and more possibilities. This ikigai quadrant focuses on what you can be paid for, emphasizing the balance between your passionate pursuits and financial sustainability.

Now that you know what you love to do, and how your skills align with a worthy mission, you can begin to research the market trends and choose a niche in your industry of choice. Think about your ikigai and the lifestyle you're creating, then adapt your niche career focus to those preferences. Get online and search for people who are already experts doing what you want to do. Go straight to the top! Learn psychology, storytelling, sales, and marketing skills from the best in your niche.

## What Does Your Niche Market Need Right Now?

Understanding what your niche market demands at any given moment is essential to business success. Listen to people. By staying in tune with the needs and preferences of your chosen audience, you can tailor your products or services to meet their specific needs. Add value to their lives by solving a problem, or making something better.

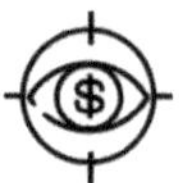

You possess knowledge and skills right now that equate tremendous value to someone in the world. There is something that you love, and that you are great at, that can create economic value in the marketplace today. Once you know what you're best at, find someone that NEEDS what YOU have to offer. Money is created as a result of delivering value to others. You are valuable!

In terms of your business or profession, your goals might include increasing revenue, expanding your customer base, improving content, or launching a new product or service. It could also involve improving your skills or knowledge in a particular area through professional development opportunities or networking. Whatever your goals are, you can integrate your ikigai to create more synchronicity and success at work. Ask WHY questions. Observing the market and asking yourself "WHY?" will always give you fresh business insights and may even make you aware of lucrative new opportunities.

For you, the point of engaging in any business, job, or career should be to have fun doing something you love, while helping other people AND making money. Integrating your passions with the right career or entrepreneurial venture will create a lifestyle that you never need a vacation from. Many individuals from various walks of life have embraced ikigai and allowed its principles to transform their destinies. I did it and millions of others have created massive success by adopting the process of ikigai. You can do it too!

Consider the story of Bridget, a corporate sales professional turned social entrepreneur. Fueled by her passion for sustainable living and a deep-seated desire to address environmental issues, Bridget manifested her dreams by founding a company that produces eco-friendly products. She also donates a portion of the company's profits to a tree-planting charity. Her endeavor not only aligns with her values, but also contributes meaningfully to the global need for jobs, new trees, and sustainable business practices.

Another example is Thomas, a software developer who realized that his true passion lay in education and empowering others. By using ikigai to align his skills with his love for teaching, he discovered his sense of purpose as an online coding instructor. Thomas quit his unfulfilling office job and became a full-time coach and content creator, replacing his 9-5 job. Now his online business generates 10X the amount of his old salary!

Thomas and Bridget both exemplify how ikigai can guide a shift in career paths, leading to a more fun, fulfilling, and rewarding life. We call this type of experience an **ABUNDANCE ALERT**!

Changing careers will require you to undergo an identity shift. For ikigai to work effectively you must commit 100% to owning your new identity. This will involve new thinking patterns, going to new places, exploring new opportunities, networking with like-minded individuals, and constant learning. Study people who already have what you desire to create. Connect with them, learn from them. Being outspoken and confident in your WHY will attract the right people to you. Go for what you want. Be a Star!

Use the internet to increase your income. Search on Google and YouTube for people to uplift. Who has problems that YOU can help them solve? Join communities, reach out, and offer your expertise. Put yourself out there as the expert in your niche and add consistent value to people's lives. Build a personal brand around your WHY and make money doing what you love to do. Create more abundance. You deserve the BEST that life has to offer!

What is your niche industry?

------------------------------------------------------------

------------------------------------------------------------

What opportunities do you see in the marketplace?

------------------------------------------------------------

------------------------------------------------------------

What's the most fulfilling way to monetize your skills?

------------------------------------------------------------

------------------------------------------------------------

WHY?

------------------------------------------------------------

------------------------------------------------------------

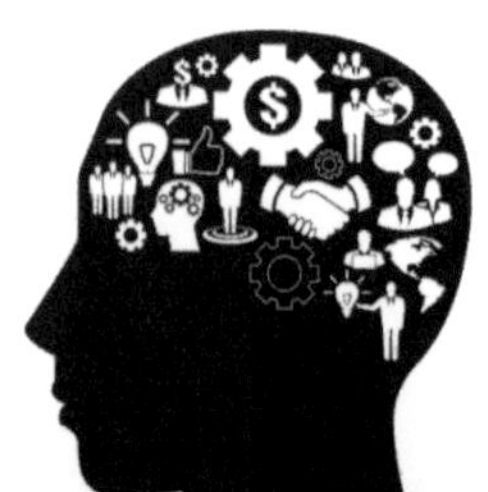

# How To Complete Your Ikigai

Many people know of ikigai as "the Japanese secret to a fulfilling life." It's all about deciding your WHY, and discovering where these **'4 Qualities of Life'** intersect.

1. **What you LOVE:** The things that give you joy and light you up.
2. **What you're GOOD AT:** Your talents, skills, and natural abilities.
3. **What the world NEEDS:** Big challenges that you feel drawn to solve, and ways you want to contribute your abundance to the world. How can you make people's lives better with your natural gifts? Think big!
4. **What you can be PAID FOR:** Get paid to do what you love. How can you sustain yourself, make an abundant living, and connect your passion to people's needs?

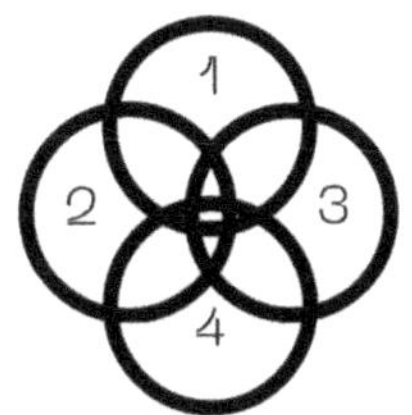

1. **Draw Your Map:** The ikigai map is a diagram composed of four overlapping circles labeled with the 4 quadrants from above. I've included a blank map for you as well as an example of my completed ikigai map.
2. **Brainstorm:** For each circle, write down everything that comes to mind: hobbies, causes that matter to you, talents that people comment on, and your dream career. Don't limit yourself, the bigger the better!
    - Look for Overlaps: See where ideas in the different circles start to connect.
    - **Passion** = Intersection of "Love" and "Good At"
    - **Purpose** = "Love" and "World Needs"
    - **People** = "World Needs" and "Paid For"
    - **Profession** = "Paid For" and "Good At"
3. **Decide What Completes Your Ikigai:** This is what goes in the center of your map, where ALL the circles connect. Don't worry if this takes time to reveal itself, your desires and goals can change. Stay in the flow and write every day to develop awareness and focus.

# Crafting Your Purpose Statement

Your 'Purpose Statement" is like a one-sentence mission statement, or a short description of what fuels your actions and gives meaning to your life. It's your WHY.

Here's a recipe to craft your Purpose Statement:
1. **What's Your Ikigai?**: What themes emerge from your map? What stands out to you across the circles?
2. **Start With a Verb:** "To inspire...", "To build..", "To create..." These words give your statement energy.
   ◦ Who, What, and WHY:
      ▪ Who are you? Who do you want to help/what issue do you want to address? WHY?
   ◦ What do you want to provide them with?
   ◦ WHY is this important to you? WHY do you care?
   ◦ Affirm your belief with I AM affirmations.
3. **Stay in the Flow!** You don't have to nail it perfectly on the first try — refining it over time is normal.

# Purpose Keys

**Narrow Your Focus**
- A powerful purpose statement doesn't try to solve everything. Which opportunity compels you the most? Be specific. Ask WHY? Clarify your focus. (Example: Instead of "Help the planet", try "Advocate for responsible water use in my local community.")

**Impact Verbs**
- Use strong verbs that convey the change you want to create: "ignite", "uplift", and "transform" can be stronger than generic helping verbs. What do you do?

**Make It Yours**
- Forget trying to sound impressive. A simple but heartfelt statement from YOU is better than an inauthentic, borrowed one. Write your purpose statement like you'd say it to a friend. Own your WHY.

**Purpose is Your Compass**
- Your ikigai shows you what's possible. Your purpose statement acts as a compass, guiding your focused decisions to win. Purpose is how you find meaning, not just in your WHY, but by contributing value to others.

# IKIGAI

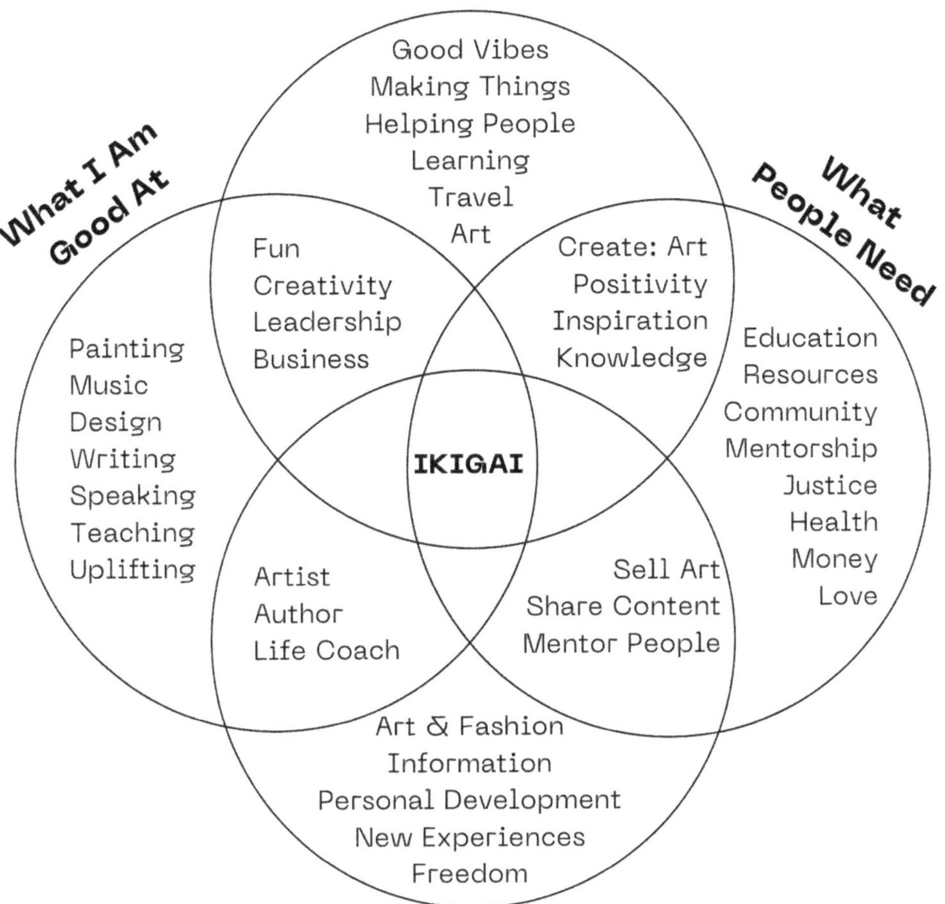


**I AM AN ARTIST, AUTHOR, AND CLARITY COACH
UPLIFTING THE WORLD WITH ALL OF MY GOD-GIVEN GIFTS**

This is my ikigai. Everything is based on my WHY.
I used to feel lost, confused, and unsure of my future until I got crystal clear on my WHY. I discovered how to use ikigai to stay focused, organized, and disciplined. Now, I live my dream life. I am a full-time artist, author, and clarity coach. I also founded We Uplift The World, an arts education company that empowers creative entrepreneurs. I get to travel the world helping people and sharing my art. Life's great. Praise GOD!

# WHAT IS YOUR IKIGAI?

Complete Your Ikigai Map & Purpose Statement

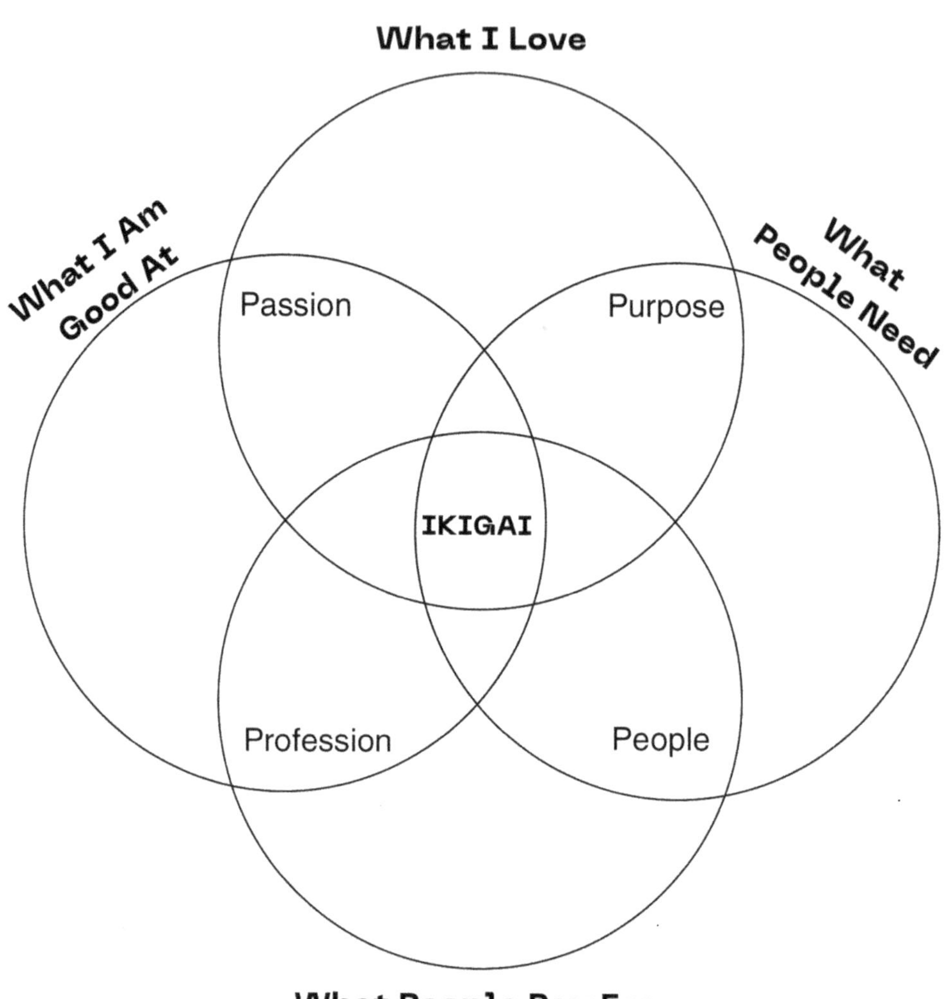


MY PURPOSE STATEMENT

# CLARIFY YOUR IKIGAI

I am so happy and grateful now that I finally
discovered ________________________________.
(True Purpose, Your WHY)

I am a _____________________ that helps people
(Who Are You?)

to _________________ by _____________________.
(What You Help People Do)     (How You Help People Do It)

I Love My Life! My lifestyle is ________________.
(Your New Lifestyle)

Every day I get to _____________________ and it
(Your New Activities)

makes me feel so ______________________________.
(Your New Feelings)

I'm leaving a legacy of __________________________.
(What Is Your Legacy?)

I am winning in life because I choose to be a
winner! I know my WHY, I am living my purpose,
and I'm creating the most abundant future.
PRAISE GOD!

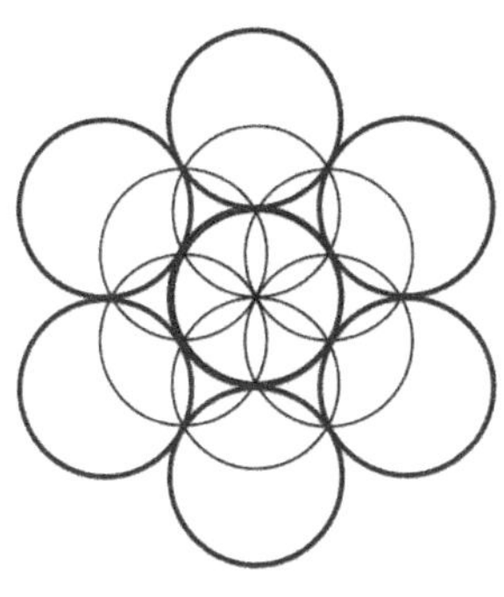

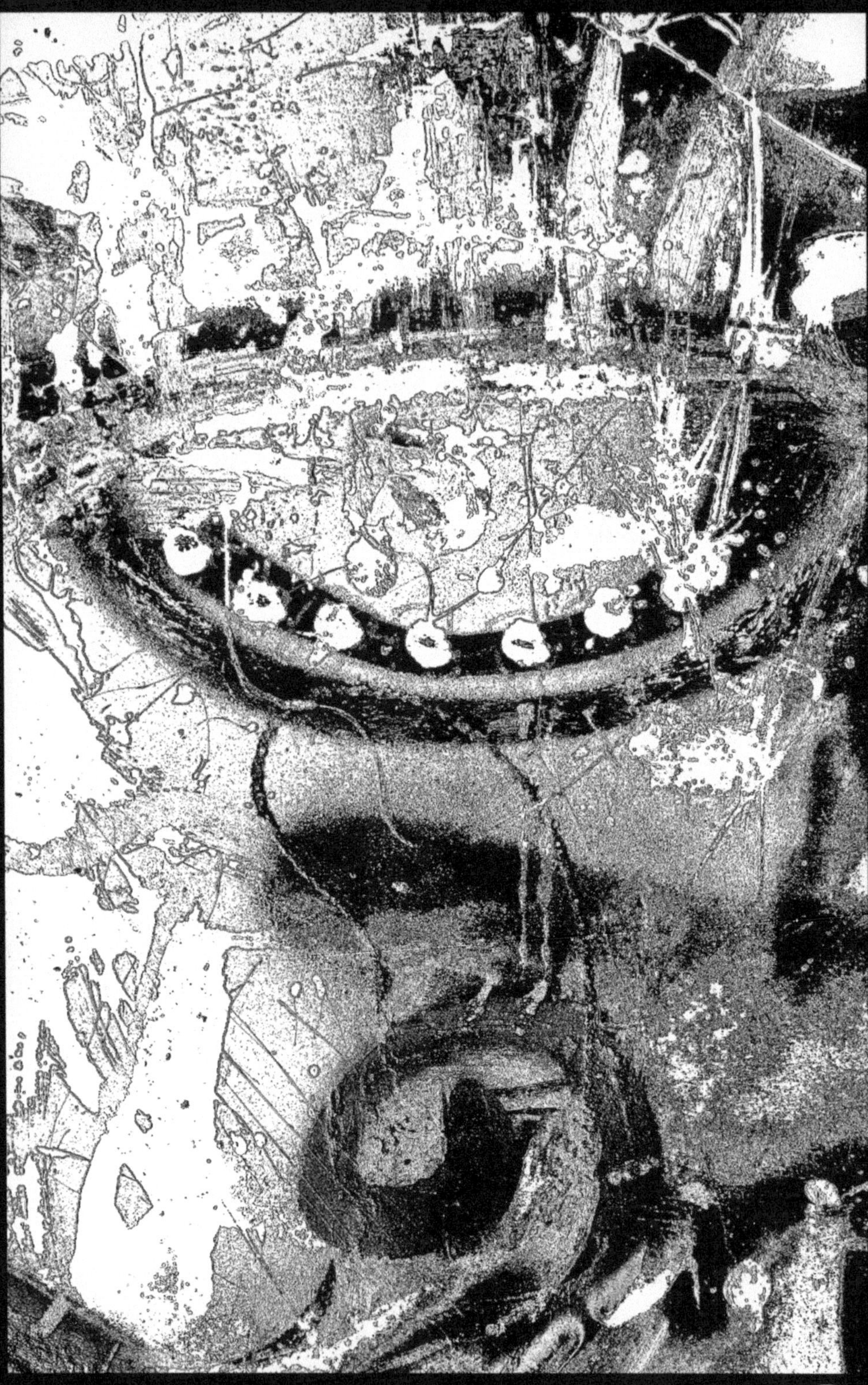
Bijan Machen ©
WHY?

# SUCCESS IS A JOURNEY, NOT A DESTINATION

As you move through life, situations, circumstances, and experiences will influence your mind to believe certain things about yourself and the world. I used to believe it was me AGAINST the world, that everyone was my competition. I also used to pessimistically believe in "Murphy's Law". None of these ideas supported my growth or made me feel good. These were society's false programs that I picked up during my childhood, and it was the wrong mentality to have. I've changed my mind.

The truth is that YOU CAN have a life where everything goes your way, where things just work out in your favor. Whether you realize it now or not, every experience in your life is ultimately a good one. Every situation or circumstance you've endured can be used for good. Even if it seems like a bad thing now, you must trust that every experience will ultimately work for the benefit of you and others. It is imperative that you view everything as a great situation and keep moving forward with positive expectations. You will get what you expect. Expect the best!

GOD loves you! All the forces of the universe are conspiring to bring you everything you desire. What you want, wants you! Situations aren't "just happening to you." Life happens FOR you, not TO you. Remember to stay in the light. Be courageous, be confident, and maintain your belief in the highest, best, Super Star version of yourself. Be it until you become it!

Your journey will likely be full of ups & downs, twists & turns, and unexpected surprises that can take you on a rollercoaster ride of emotions. It's all good. Smile, learn fast, and apply every lesson. You will experience transformations that encourage you to achieve more. Embrace the challenges that come your way, for they are opportunities to grow and become a better version of yourself. Focus on what you can control in the present moment and appreciate your personal development journey. Enjoy the now.

**REMINDER:** Success is not about reaching a final destination, it's about enjoying your journey & learning from every experience along the way. You are doing your best! Each day is a new adventure for you to enjoy. Keep a positive, optimistic mindset and choose the best feeling energy. Use discernment, and trust your intuition.
VIBES!

If you don't like something about your experience, you can always change it now. I've been in plenty of jobs, friendships, and relationships that I had to transition out of. Always remain true to your values, true to your desires, and true to your WHY. You will know when it's time to make a change in your life. Don't procrastinate. Once you KNOW, it's time to GO!

Life is too awesome to be unhappy or miserable with the way you're living. If there's something you're not happy about in your life, it's important to remember that you have the power to make an immediate shift. Whether it's a job you don't like, a relationship that's not working out, or a habit that's holding you back, you can take control of your life and make a change for the better.

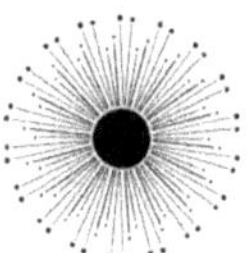

You have to own your own happiness. Your ability to be happy is an inside job, independent from any other person or outside influence. You CAN transform your life's circumstances, but you must first make the deliberate decision to 'feel good now.' When you know and live your WHY, you feel good, and when you stay aligned with your ikigai, the increased confidence in your purpose will guide you toward abundant success.

Do not settle for a lifestyle that doesn't bring you great purpose, joy, and fulfillment. Take the necessary steps to create the life you know you deserve. You might encounter obstacles along the way, but with the right tools, a clear focus, determination, and perseverance, you can overcome anything and achieve your goals.

You are the master of your fate and the captain of your soul! So if there's anything in your life that you're not abundantly happy with, don't be afraid to change it now. You have the power to transform your situation and create a beautiful lifestyle that you love. Just do it!

When you focus your thoughts on a specific outcome or desire, your brain naturally fixates on it, leading to an obsession. Placing this desire on a pedestal creates a distance between you and the goal. Unbeknownst to you, you end up chasing it, causing it to move further away. To counter this, you need to believe that the thing you desire is attainable and that you deserve it.  Focus on making winning decisions and taking the actions required to achieve the goal, visualizing your winning results. Acting 'as if' you already possess your desires will magnetize them to you faster. If you were living the life of your dreams right now, what would you be doing? Act 'as if' you're already doing it. By consistently taking purposeful actions, you'll bring the desired outcome closer to you, creating success. Thoughts create reality.

**EXAMPLE:** Say you're in car sales and you want to buy your own Lambo. Envision yourself talking to happy customers and making enough successful cold calls to sell 1,000 cars. Focus on improving your communication skills and taking massive action to manifest the Lamborghini, don't just hope for it. Instead of idolizing the end goal, concentrate on enhancing the key skills that will ultimately bring you closer to it. You will make your dreams come true by creating them deliberately. Enjoy the process of creating. What will you create next?

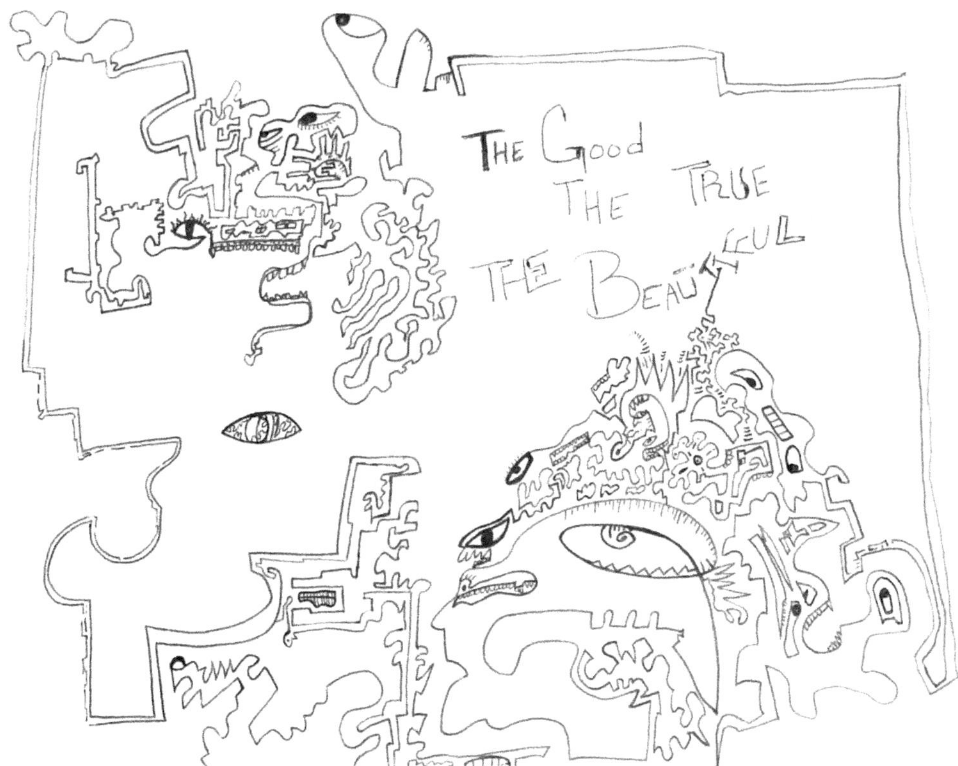

Reflect on the essence of who you are without considering the opinions of other people or any societal programs you may have encountered earlier in life. Societal programs are deeply ingrained belief systems, social structures, and thought patterns that often shape our perceptions and influence decisions. False programs can include sayings like "you're nobody special", "life is so hard" or "being rich is impossible". Most of the programs at play in society are negative and do not benefit your success, they actually try to hook your energy, distract you, and hold you back.

Recognizing these negative programs is essential for freeing yourself and manifesting your ideal reality. By breaking free from doubt, fear, and societal programs, you'll open yourself up to new possibilities and great opportunities for personal growth. No matter what you've experienced in the past, you can always change your life by choosing a new program to subscribe to. Create more than you consume. Stop scrolling on social media, turn off the television, and create your own abundance program.

# REMEMBER

- You can be, do, and have anything you desire!
- Believe and you receive. Doubt and you'll go without.
- Be open, be teachable, and be coachable.
- Have a high teachability index (high willingness to learn + high willingness to accept change).
- Train your brain every day with a good mental diet (books, videos, podcasts, LAMBO MACH music).
- Your income will equal the average of your 5 best friends. Choose to be around winners & go-getters.
- Honor your WHY and live your ikigai. Love what you do and you'll never work a day in your life.
- Put something on the calendar! Life is more fun when you have something to look forward to. Schedule wins.
- Be courageous and never afraid! Fear is a lie. You can do anything. You are a powerful child of GOD!
- People either build up or destroy. Be a builder.
- Leaders are always writers and readers. Be a Leader.
- Actions speak louder than words. Take action.
- The Winners Always Win. YOU ARE A WINNER!

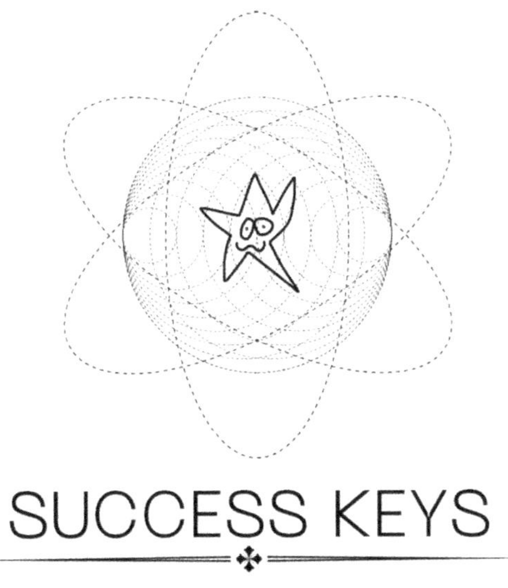

# SUCCESS KEYS

- **Be True to You:** It's tempting to focus on what others say you should do, but stay true to your vision. Be you!

- **Keep it Visual:** Put your ikigai map somewhere you'll see it often. That way, you can stay inspired and make updates whenever you feel. Practice visualizing yourself winning. See success in your mind's eye. See yourself having it, then feel the feelings of having all that you desire right now.

- **Depth of Vision:** Discovering and living your ikigai is an ongoing process, not a single event. Visualize the long-term impact of your words and actions. See it now.

- **Now** is the time for growth and self-discovery. Don't stress if it's not crystal clear right away. Just focus on what you can control now and keep moving forward.

- **Focus** on doing things that bring you joy and a sense of meaning. You CAN do it all, but not all at once. FOCUS!

- **Talk to people** you admire! Ask what it took for them to become great. What are their success habits? How did they find their purpose? You might be surprised.

- **Live your ikigai** every day in small moments, not just grand ambitions. It can be the difference between doing boring homework vs. passionately researching a topic that truly interests you, knowing that this experience is contributing to your overall greatness.

- **Start From Where You Are.** Be grateful for where you're at and appreciate how far you've come in life. Focus on progress while enjoying the process of living your ikigai, rather than waiting around for your life to miraculously change. Take one step at a time and use your past you propel you forward. Your future is bright!

- **Free Your Mind.** Release yourself from your ego, expectations, and judgments, and embrace your authentic self. Tune in to the energy of abundance. Relax your mind. Be still. Breathe. You are free now.

- **Harmonize.** Living in sustainable harmony means respecting your environment, the community, and yourself while creating a graceful balance between everything. As you create, be at peace with all that is.

- **Appreciate Every Detail.** Make it your priority to find happiness in the simple pleasures of life, such as a good cup of tea, pets, nature, or a smile from a stranger. Enjoy every beautiful detail of your life.

- **Be Here Now.** Being in the here and now means living in the present moment, without dwelling on the past or worrying about the future. You are enjoying the now, as you deliberately create your future.  It's easier to be present and peaceful when you're living your ikigai.

- **Share Your Ikigai.** Inspire and uplift others by sharing your passion, purpose, and gifts with the world. Use the internet to connect with people.  Your awareness and mastery will increase when you use your unique talents to make a positive impact on those around you. Your gifts are meant to be shared and celebrated.

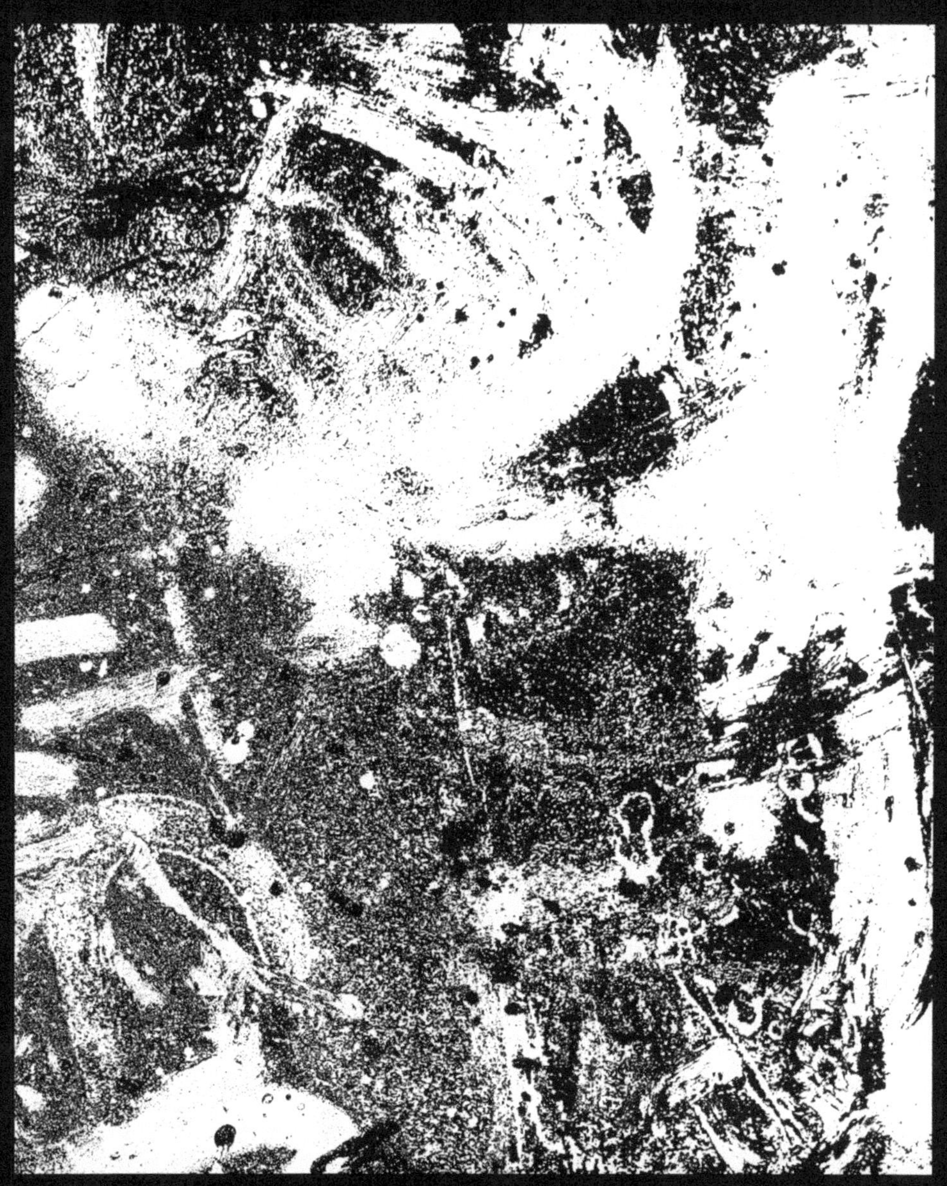

When you have a new idea, write it down and take action on it IMMEDIATELY! Be courageous enough to act on your intuition. (That's GOD speaking to you) The creative act of writing will accelerate your manifestation process. The faster you take action on your plans, the faster they will come to fruition. Knowing your WHY will keep you focused and motivated to uplift more people. Shine bright! You are a Super Star!

# The Power of Daily Writing

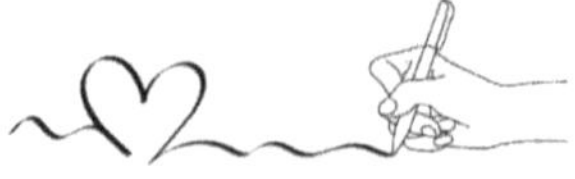

Daily writing is an essential tool that will help you excel in many ways. Writing helps you express your thoughts, words, and emotions clearly. It will also improve your awareness. Writing every day will help you to be more organized and focused, providing structure and routine to your life. Write down everything you want to be, do, and have, then create a system to get it. Systems create wins.

Writing can be a form of therapy, helping you to reduce stress and anxiety by improving the way you feel as you release your emotions onto the page. It will also help you gain perspective on current life situations so you can create solutions. Write more often to de-clutter your mind, decide the best next steps, and plan more wins.

Go to your journal when you want to improve your mental and emotional well-being, as well as your professional productivity. Ideas will flow through your mind all day, every day. Keep your mind clear by writing. Remember to write down all of your good-feeling thoughts and review them daily.

Creative writing & drawing will significantly expand your imagination, making you more aware of your potential. What are the best things you can imagine for yourself? By putting your thoughts down on paper, you will free up space in your mind to explore fresh ideas while you develop new perspectives and plans to achieve your predetermined success. Having a vivid imagination will accelerate the speed of your manifestations.

Once you commit to a decision, stick to it! Consistent dedication to improving your habits will take you exactly where you want to go. Set aside a specific time each day to write your thoughts and plans for the future.

**MY WRITING TIME IS:**_________________________________________

# PROSPERITY PROCESS

1. Enhance your transformation process by writing down new goals for your health, career, and lifestyle. Once you successfully achieve a goal, you will create better habits and systems to reach bigger goals.

2. Emphasize engaging in activities that enhance well-being, establish achievable business goals for prosperity, and prioritize physical health through a balanced diet and a consistent exercise routine.

3. Visualize the path to your desired future as you set your sights on the remainder of the year. Envision a fun, holistic approach to your ikigai-based improvement plan. Envision the most ideal version of you, your "Super Star Self". Reflect on what truly matters to you, your legacy, and how you can make meaningful progress toward your aspirations. Visualize it. You can be, do, and have anything and everything you desire!

4. Consolidate your big goals into bite-sized, actionable steps, creating a roadmap that leads you to abundant success. Stay motivated by celebrating ALL victories along the way and adjusting your course as needed. Remember, success is a journey, and each step forward is a testament to your dedication.

5. As you clarify your goals for the next day, week, month, and year, remember to be kind to yourself and practice self-care. Cultivate a supportive environment that nurtures your growth and fuels your ambition. With determination and a clear vision in mind, you are well-equipped to manifest the bright future that awaits you.

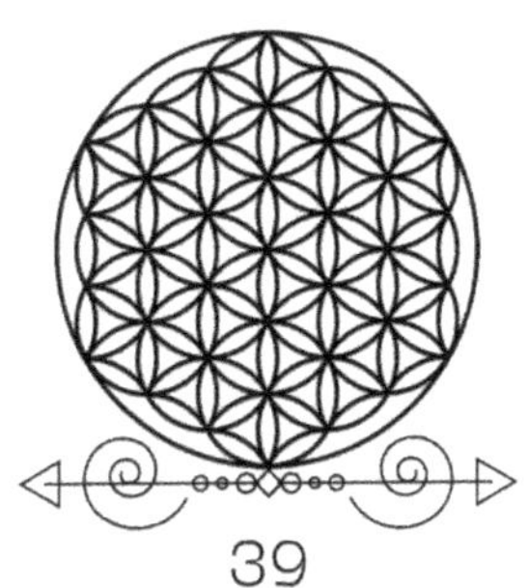

# CLARITY QUESTIONS

Ask yourself these WHY questions to improve clarity & awareness.
Be kind, patient, and honest with yourself.

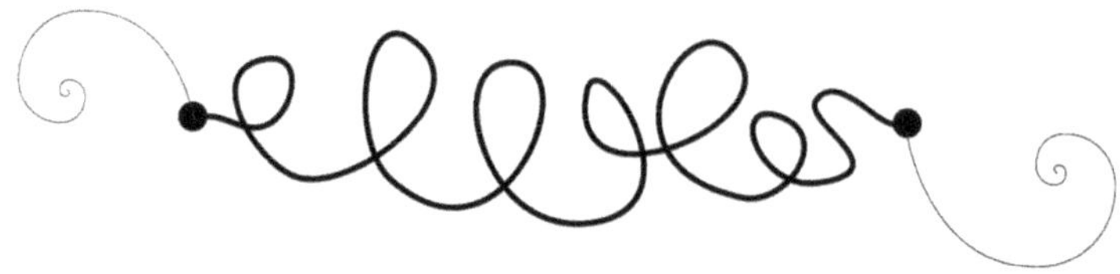

### What is your WHY?

- WHY is your WHY, your WHY? Keep asking WHY

- ______________________________________________

  ______________________________________________

  ______________________________________________

### What makes you feel good?

- List the activities that bring you good feelings.

- ______________________________________________

  ______________________________________________

  ______________________________________________

### Who is the highest version of you?

- Describe your Super Star Self. Start with "I Am"...

- ______________________________________________

  ______________________________________________

  ______________________________________________

### What emotions do you enjoy feeling the most?

- WHY do you love feeling this way?

- ______________________________________________

  ______________________________________________

  ______________________________________________

**What activity do you absolutely love?**

- What do you enjoy doing so much that you could do it every day without quitting? WHY?

- ________________________________________________

  ________________________________________________

  ________________________________________________

**Which talents do you believe in the most?**

- What do you KNOW you are great at doing?

- ________________________________________________

  ________________________________________________

  ________________________________________________

**What are your core values?**

- What do you stand for? What's important to you?

- ________________________________________________

  ________________________________________________

  ________________________________________________

**What is your destiny?**

- You create your future. Where are you going?

- ________________________________________________

  ________________________________________________

  ________________________________________________

**What is your legacy?**

- What will you be remembered for? WHY?

- ________________________________________________

  ________________________________________________

  ________________________________________________

By taking the time to complete your ikigai and articulate your WHY, you gain confidence through creating mental clarity, empowering you to focus on the things that matter most to you, resulting in the achievement of your chief aim. It also helps to have a plan with a schedule to commit to. You will win more abundantly by creating simple, detailed action plans that move your life forward every day. You have everything you need, just take the next step.

On the next few pages, you will find a collection of planners and awareness activities. The planners include sections for dates, goals, and action steps. Completing these habitually will help you to develop clear plans for achieving success and make you a consistent winner.

When filling out your planner, it is important to focus on the things that bring you the most alignment, joy, and fulfillment, considering how living your WHY will benefit others. Don't be limited by your past or current circumstances. By approaching your purpose with a mindset of optimism and compassion, you will create a more meaningful life for yourself and those around you. Stay true to your vision, take action, and expect the best!

Prepare for abundant success. You're a winner. Expect to win. Organize your day by reserving time to fill out your planner at night before bed or first thing in the morning. Enjoy the process. By writing daily, you'll gain clarity, focus, and a sense of purpose that will empower you to create the life that you've always dreamed of. It's Manifestation SZN!

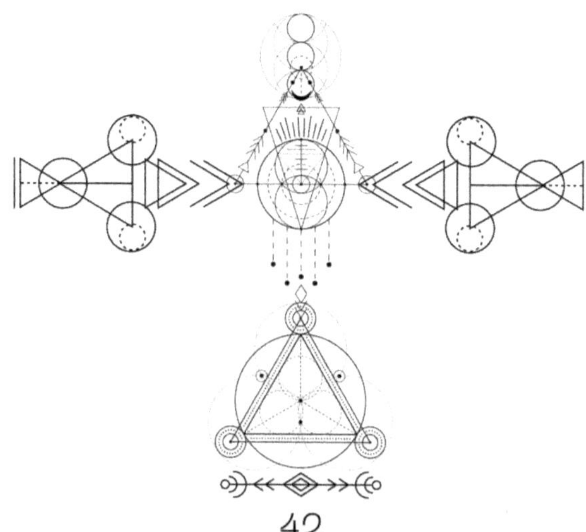

# 30 Days of Self+Awareness

| MON | TUES | WED | THUR | FRI |
|---|---|---|---|---|
| Take a 33-minute mindful walk | Write down 13 things you're grateful for | Try something new | Spend 33 minutes meditating | Listen to the ABUNDANCE UNIVERSE podcast |
| Practice deep breathing for 9 minutes | Call or meet a friend for a heart-to-heart talk | Take a break from your mobile phone for the entire day | Cook a healthy meal for yourself | Learn 1 new skill on YouTube |
| Visit a park or natural reserve | Text message 3 people "Thank You" | Listen to LAMBO MACH music | Do a random act of kindness | Say "No" to a commitment you're not excited about |
| Write about a happy memory | Try a new hobby or revisit an old one | Watch a cool documentary | Go to bed an hour earlier | Do something fun & spontaneous |
| Buy yourself a $3 gift | Read a good book | Try a new tea or smoothie flavor | Spend 33 minutes in the sun | Write down 13 things you love about yourself |
| Give something away to a friend or stranger | Write in your journal for 33 minutes | Massage Your Hands & Feet | Do something creative | Reflect on the progress you've made this month |

**You can add these to your phone calendar and set reminders!**

# THE ABUNDANCE WHEEL

The Abundance Wheel is a clarity tool that helps you to better understand what you can do to make your life more abundant. Think about the 8 life categories below, and rate them from 1 – 10. Assess where you are right now and decide where you want to be. Use your planner to map out different things that will move you closer to your goals. Take small steps to improve every day and you will get to where you want to be in life.
Let's manifest an **ABUNDANCE ALERT**!

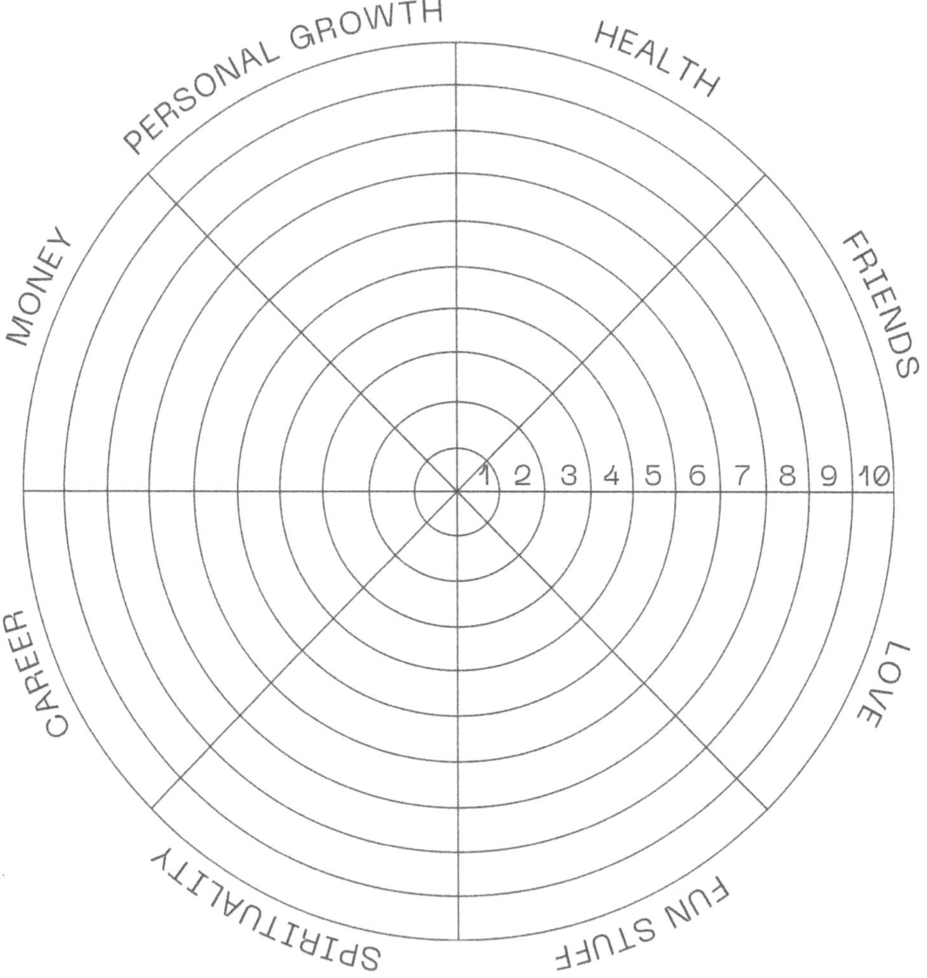


Health + Friends + Love + Fun + Spirituality + Career + Money + Growth

# You Are Successful

no matter where you come from
whether you have lots of money or no money,
no matter how many negative experiences or
challenges you've had in the past,
you can create a life of abundance now
you are successful!

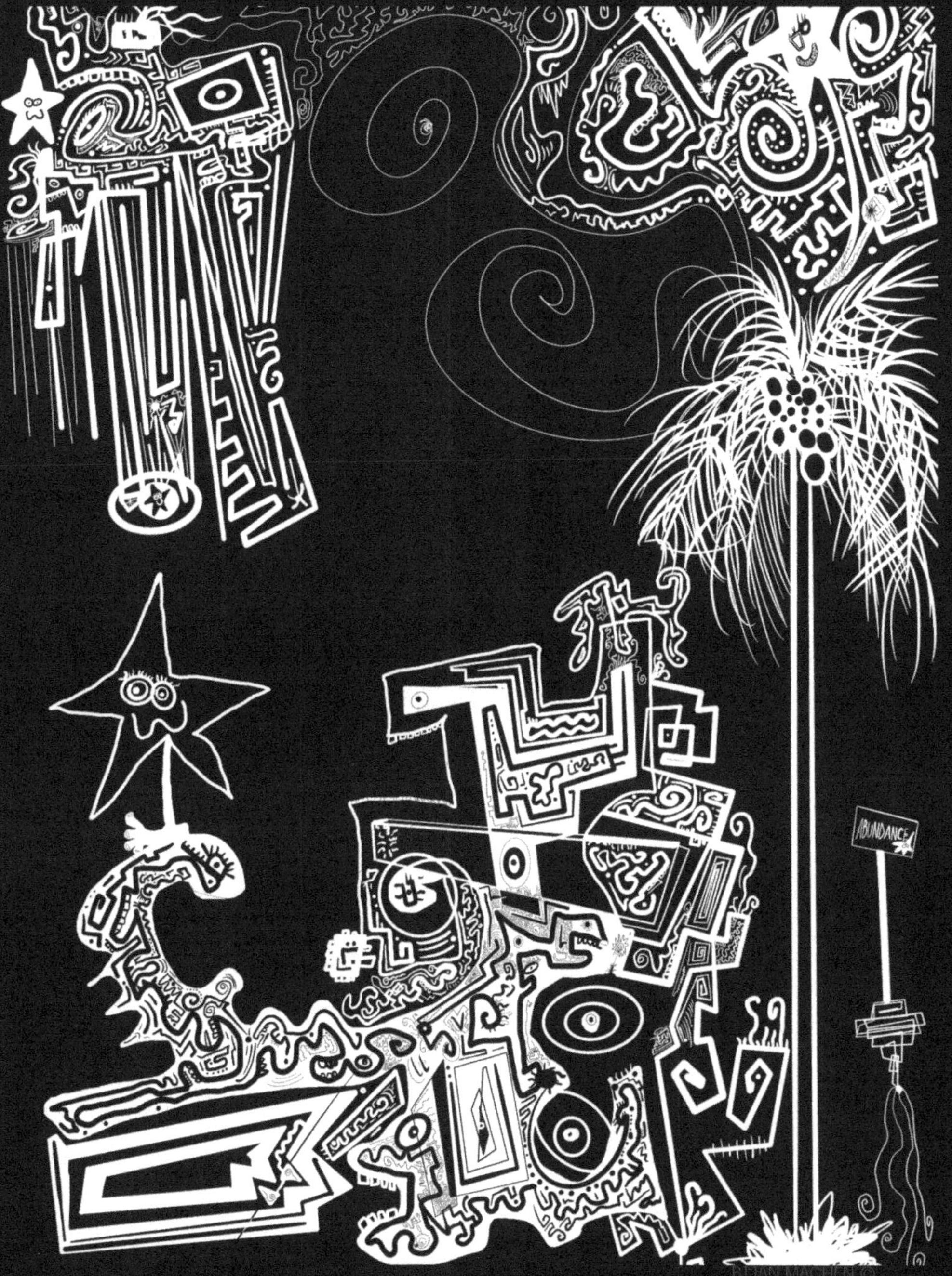

# IKIGAI GOALS

Setting goals that align with your ikigai will ensure that you are working towards achieving your desired outcomes. Regarding lifestyle, business, and health, it's important to set achievable yet challenging goals that will push you to be your best self. Your goals should build upon your ikigai and your WHY, resulting in you being more peaceful, positive, productive, and progressive.

When it comes to improving your health, you can set goals related to exercise, diet, and nutrition, such as incorporating more whole foods into your meals or reducing your intake of sugar and processed foods. Can you exercise more often? Or drink a gallon of water today?

Prioritize getting more sleep, reducing stress, and committing to a regular exercise routine that aligns with your interests and fitness level. You might consider setting goals related to spiritual self-care, such as incorporating more daily prayer, meditation, or nature time into your routine, and making time for creative activities that bring you joy.

You can also focus on building healthy relationships with loved ones and developing a stronger sense of community through joining groups of like-minded individuals that align with your values. Use the internet to create, connect, and make your dreams come true! Sharing your gifts with the world more abundantly will bring you clarity, fulfillment, and purpose.

**How will you use your ikigai to achieve new goals?**

Write down 3 ikigai goals. Choose 1 to complete by next week, 1 next month, and 1 to achieve by next year.

Week:_________________________________________________

Month:________________________________________________

Year:_________________________________________________

# SET SMART GOALS

Setting SMART goals—Specific, Measurable, Achievable, Relevant, and Time-bound—is crucial for success. Specific goals clarify objectives. Measurable goals track progress. Achievable goals maintain belief. Relevant goals align with values, and Time-bound goals create urgency. Develop SMART goals for yourself. Focus on the process, not just the outcome. Build a simple, step-by-step system to achieve each of your SMART goals.

## EXAMPLE

Specific — What do I want to accomplish and why?

Measurable — How will I know when I have accomplished it?

Achievable — Do I believe that I can accomplish this goal right now?

Relevant — Is now the right time for me to be working towards this goal?

Timebound — When do I want to accomplish this goal by?

## Goal 1:

Specific.

Measurable.

Achievable.

Relevant.

Timebound.

## Goal 2:

Specific.

Measurable.

Achievable.

Relevant.

Timebound.

## Goal 3:

Specific.

Measurable.

Achievable.

Relevant.

Timebound.

# Self-Awareness Questions

This is a fun awareness reflection that you can do anytime to remind yourself of your WHY. Answer these questions honestly, and without judgment. When you arrive at a response for each question, ask WHY? Be as clear as possible and feel free to write responses in your journal if you need more space. Be yourself!

Who do I choose to be? --- _______________________

What are my strengths? --- _______________________

What do I love about myself? _______________________

Who matters the most to me? _______________________

What am I proud of? ------ _______________________

What do I like to do for fun? _______________________

What am I afraid of? ----- _______________________

What is my dream? ------- _______________________

What gets me excited? --- _______________________

What brings me the most joy? _______________________

What keeps me grounded? -- _______________________

What am I grateful for? ---- _______________________

What are my values? ------- _______________________

When do I feel my best? ---- _______________________

What is my WHY? --------- _______________________

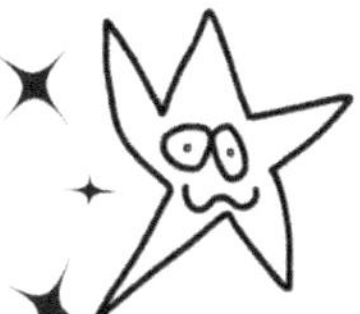

# PURPOSE PLANNER

Create an Action Plan to align each area of your life with your purpose. Everything you do should lead to personal growth, achievement, fulfillment, and purposeful success.

**Purpose Statement:**

| Personal Goals | Action Plan |
| --- | --- |
| | |

| Work Goals | Action Plan |
| --- | --- |
| | |

| Health Goals | Action Plan |
| --- | --- |
| | |

| Financial Goals | Action Plan |
| --- | --- |
| | |

**New Habits To Develop:**

# DAILY PLANNER



AFFIRMATION:

## I AM GRATEFUL FOR

| TOP 3 PRIORITIES |
| --- |

1 ______________________

2 ______________________

3 ______________________

| TASK LIST |
| --- |

- ______________________
- ______________________
- ______________________
- ______________________
- ______________________
- ______________________
- ______________________
- ______________________

| REMEMBER |
| --- |

| TIME | SCHEDULE |
| --- | --- |
| 6:00 am | |
| 6:30 am | |
| 7:00 am | |
| 7:30 am | |
| 8:00 am | |
| 8:30 am | |
| 9:00 am | |
| 9:30 am | |
| 10:00 am | |
| 10:30 am | |
| 11:00 am | |
| 11:30 am | |
| 12:00 pm | |
| 12:30 pm | |
| 1:00 pm | |
| 1:30 pm | |
| 2:00 pm | |
| 2:30 pm | |
| 3:00 pm | |
| 3:30 pm | |
| 4:00 pm | |
| 4:30 pm | |
| 5:00 pm | |
| 5:30 pm | |
| 6:00 pm | |
| 6:30 pm | |
| 7:00 pm | |
| 7:30 pm | |
| 8:00 pm | |
| 8:30 pm | |
| 9:00 pm | |
| 9:30 pm | |
| 10:00 pm | |

# DAILY PLANNER

_________________DATE

AFFIRMATION:

_______________________________________________

_______________________________________________

## I AM GRATEFUL FOR

### TOP 3 PRIORITIES

1) _______________________________
   _______________________________

2) _______________________________
   _______________________________

3) _______________________________
   _______________________________

### TASK LIST

- ___________________________
- ___________________________
- ___________________________
- ___________________________
- ___________________________
- ___________________________
- ___________________________
- ___________________________

### REMEMBER

_______________________________

_______________________________

_______________________________

| TIME | SCHEDULE |
|---|---|
| 6:00 am | |
| 6:30 am | |
| 7:00 am | |
| 7:30 am | |
| 8:00 am | |
| 8:30 am | |
| 9:00 am | |
| 9:30 am | |
| 10:00 am | |
| 10:30 am | |
| 11:00 am | |
| 11:30 am | |
| 12:00 pm | |
| 12:30 pm | |
| 1:00 pm | |
| 1:30 pm | |
| 2:00 pm | |
| 2:30 pm | |
| 3:00 pm | |
| 3:30 pm | |
| 4:00 pm | |
| 4:30 pm | |
| 5:00 pm | |
| 5:30 pm | |
| 6:00 pm | |
| 6:30 pm | |
| 7:00 pm | |
| 7:30 pm | |
| 8:00 pm | |
| 8:30 pm | |
| 9:00 pm | |
| 9:30 pm | |
| 10:00 pm | |

# DAILY PLANNER

_______________DATE

AFFIRMATION:

## I AM GRATEFUL FOR

| TOP 3 PRIORITIES |
| --- |

1. _______________

2. _______________

3. _______________

| TASK LIST |
| --- |

- ▪
- ▪
- ▪
- ▪
- ▪
- ▪
- ▪
- ▪

| REMEMBER |
| --- |

| TIME | SCHEDULE |
| --- | --- |
| 6:00 am | |
| 6:30 am | |
| 7:00 am | |
| 7:30 am | |
| 8:00 am | |
| 8:30 am | |
| 9:00 am | |
| 9:30 am | |
| 10:00 am | |
| 10:30 am | |
| 11:00 am | |
| 11:30 am | |
| 12:00 pm | |
| 12:30 pm | |
| 1:00 pm | |
| 1:30 pm | |
| 2:00 pm | |
| 2:30 pm | |
| 3:00 pm | |
| 3:30 pm | |
| 4:00 pm | |
| 4:30 pm | |
| 5:00 pm | |
| 5:30 pm | |
| 6:00 pm | |
| 6:30 pm | |
| 7:00 pm | |
| 7:30 pm | |
| 8:00 pm | |
| 8:30 pm | |
| 9:00 pm | |
| 9:30 pm | |
| 10:00 pm | |

# DAILY PLANNER

_______________DATE

AFFIRMATION:

_______________________________________________

_______________________________________________

## I AM GRATEFUL FOR

### TOP 3 PRIORITIES

1) _______________________________
   _______________________________

2) _______________________________
   _______________________________

3) _______________________________
   _______________________________

### TASK LIST

- ____________________________________
- ____________________________________
- ____________________________________
- ____________________________________
- ____________________________________
- ____________________________________
- ____________________________________
- ____________________________________

### REMEMBER

_______________________________________

_______________________________________

_______________________________________

| TIME | SCHEDULE |
|---|---|
| 6:00 am | |
| 6:30 am | |
| 7:00 am | |
| 7:30 am | |
| 8:00 am | |
| 8:30 am | |
| 9:00 am | |
| 9:30 am | |
| 10:00 am | |
| 10:30 am | |
| 11:00 am | |
| 11:30 am | |
| 12:00 pm | |
| 12:30 pm | |
| 1:00 pm | |
| 1:30 pm | |
| 2:00 pm | |
| 2:30 pm | |
| 3:00 pm | |
| 3:30 pm | |
| 4:00 pm | |
| 4:30 pm | |
| 5:00 pm | |
| 5:30 pm | |
| 6:00 pm | |
| 6:30 pm | |
| 7:00 pm | |
| 7:30 pm | |
| 8:00 pm | |
| 8:30 pm | |
| 9:00 pm | |
| 9:30 pm | |
| 10:00 pm | |

# DAILY PLANNER

_______________DATE

AFFIRMATION:

## I AM GRATEFUL FOR

| TOP 3 PRIORITIES |
| --- |

1. _______________
   _______________
2. _______________
   _______________
3. _______________
   _______________

| TASK LIST |
| --- |

- ■ _______________
- ■ _______________
- ■ _______________
- ■ _______________
- ■ _______________
- ■ _______________
- ■ _______________
- ■ _______________

| REMEMBER |
| --- |

_______________
_______________
_______________

| TIME | SCHEDULE |
| --- | --- |
| 6:00 am | |
| 6:30 am | |
| 7:00 am | |
| 7:30 am | |
| 8:00 am | |
| 8:30 am | |
| 9:00 am | |
| 9:30 am | |
| 10:00 am | |
| 10:30 am | |
| 11:00 am | |
| 11:30 am | |
| 12:00 pm | |
| 12:30 pm | |
| 1:00 pm | |
| 1:30 pm | |
| 2:00 pm | |
| 2:30 pm | |
| 3:00 pm | |
| 3:30 pm | |
| 4:00 pm | |
| 4:30 pm | |
| 5:00 pm | |
| 5:30 pm | |
| 6:00 pm | |
| 6:30 pm | |
| 7:00 pm | |
| 7:30 pm | |
| 8:00 pm | |
| 8:30 pm | |
| 9:00 pm | |
| 9:30 pm | |
| 10:00 pm | |

# DAILY PLANNER

_______________DATE

AFFIRMATION:

## I AM GRATEFUL FOR

| | |
|---|---|
| **TOP 3 PRIORITIES** | |

1 _______________________

_______________________

2 _______________________

_______________________

3 _______________________

_______________________

**TASK LIST**

- ________________________
- ________________________
- ________________________
- ________________________
- ________________________
- ________________________
- ________________________
- ________________________

**REMEMBER**

____________________________

____________________________

____________________________

| TIME | SCHEDULE |
|---|---|
| 6:00 am | |
| 6:30 am | |
| 7:00 am | |
| 7:30 am | |
| 8:00 am | |
| 8:30 am | |
| 9:00 am | |
| 9:30 am | |
| 10:00 am | |
| 10:30 am | |
| 11:00 am | |
| 11:30 am | |
| 12:00 pm | |
| 12:30 pm | |
| 1:00 pm | |
| 1:30 pm | |
| 2:00 pm | |
| 2:30 pm | |
| 3:00 pm | |
| 3:30 pm | |
| 4:00 pm | |
| 4:30 pm | |
| 5:00 pm | |
| 5:30 pm | |
| 6:00 pm | |
| 6:30 pm | |
| 7:00 pm | |
| 7:30 pm | |
| 8:00 pm | |
| 8:30 pm | |
| 9:00 pm | |
| 9:30 pm | |
| 10:00 pm | |

# DAILY PLANNER

_______________DATE

AFFIRMATION:

## I AM GRATEFUL FOR

<table>
<tr><td>

### TOP 3 PRIORITIES

1) ___________________
___________________

2) ___________________
___________________

3) ___________________
___________________

### TASK LIST

- ___________________
- ___________________
- ___________________
- ___________________
- ___________________
- ___________________
- ___________________
- ___________________

### REMEMBER

</td><td>

| TIME | SCHEDULE |
| --- | --- |
| 6:00 am | |
| 6:30 am | |
| 7:00 am | |
| 7:30 am | |
| 8:00 am | |
| 8:30 am | |
| 9:00 am | |
| 9:30 am | |
| 10:00 am | |
| 10:30 am | |
| 11:00 am | |
| 11:30 am | |
| 12:00 pm | |
| 12:30 pm | |
| 1:00 pm | |
| 1:30 pm | |
| 2:00 pm | |
| 2:30 pm | |
| 3:00 pm | |
| 3:30 pm | |
| 4:00 pm | |
| 4:30 pm | |
| 5:00 pm | |
| 5:30 pm | |
| 6:00 pm | |
| 6:30 pm | |
| 7:00 pm | |
| 7:30 pm | |
| 8:00 pm | |
| 8:30 pm | |
| 9:00 pm | |
| 9:30 pm | |
| 10:00 pm | |

</td></tr>
</table>

# TASK ASSESSMENT CHECKLIST

Refine your current work life. What can you change at your job to create more joy and fulfillment? Start by carefully analyzing how you spend each minute while completing tasks each day. By organizing your work efficiently, you can align your responsibilities with your WHY, and live your ikigai.

| DATE & TIME | TASK DESCRIPTION | TIME SPENT ON THIS TASK | HOW DO I FEEL PERFORMING THE TASK? WHY? | WHO AM I CONNECTING WITH? WHY? |
|---|---|---|---|---|
|  |  |  |  |  |
|  |  |  |  |  |
|  |  |  |  |  |
|  |  |  |  |  |
|  |  |  |  |  |
|  |  |  |  |  |
|  |  |  |  |  |

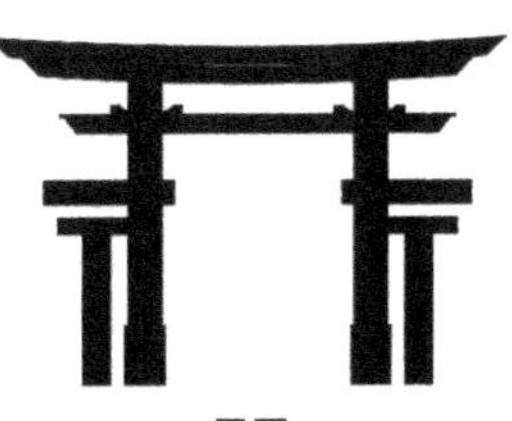

# Weekly Awareness Reflection

Consistent reflection will bring you clarity and increased self-awareness. Feel free to copy this page in your personal journal and review it often.

## TOP 3 ACCOMPLISHMENTS THIS WEEK

- ☐
- ☐
- ☐

**I AM GRATEFUL FOR**

**I NOTICED MYSELF BEING**

**LESSONS LEARNED**

**HOW CAN I GET MORE DONE?**

**WHAT HABITS DO I WANT TO CHANGE?**

**THE BEST THING ABOUT THIS WEEK WAS**

# KEYS TO YOUR LIVING WHY

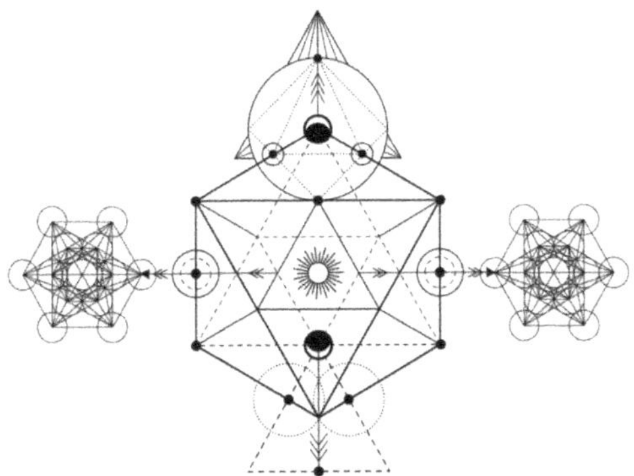

- **Create.** Create more than you consume. Never criticize other people or yourself. Use the four questions of ikigai to create new opportunities that are aligned with your talents, passions, and values. You are a creator!
- **Stay Open.** Experiment with different ways of expressing your ikigai and use what works for you. Choose the best feeling vibes and focus on creativity.
- **Be Real.** Balance your ikigai with your current needs, wants, and obligations to prioritize your daily activities. Be honest about your desires. Live life!
- **Gratitude is GOLD.** Always be grateful for what you have right now. The high vibrational energy of gratitude will fuel you to enthusiastically create the life you desire. Say "PRAISE GOD" for everything!
- **Connect.** Talk to more people. Share your ikigai with other people and inspire them to shine their light!
- **Celebrate Life.** Celebrate your achievements no matter how big or small.  Appreciate your entire journey. You are a unique Super Star destined for greatness!

Spend more time self-reflecting and writing every day to accelerate your personal growth. Stay positive, have fun, and prioritize the things that make you 'feel good now'. The next few pages include some blank ikigai maps. You can update or expand your ikigai anytime you need more clarity. Life is always evolving for you so naturally, your aspirations will change. Prioritize what feeds you. Stay in the flow!

# WHAT IS YOUR IKIGAI?

Complete Your Ikigai Map & Purpose Statement

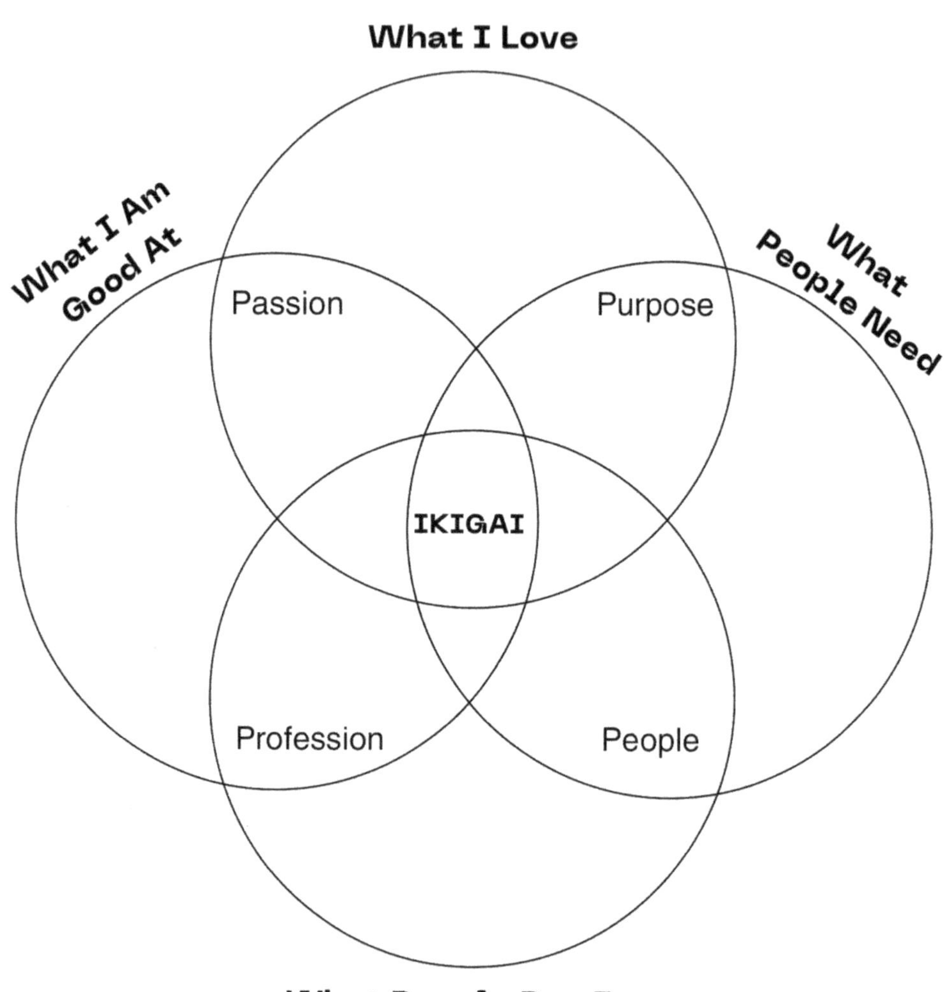


MY PURPOSE STATEMENT

# WHAT IS YOUR IKIGAI?

Complete Your Ikigai Map & Purpose Statement

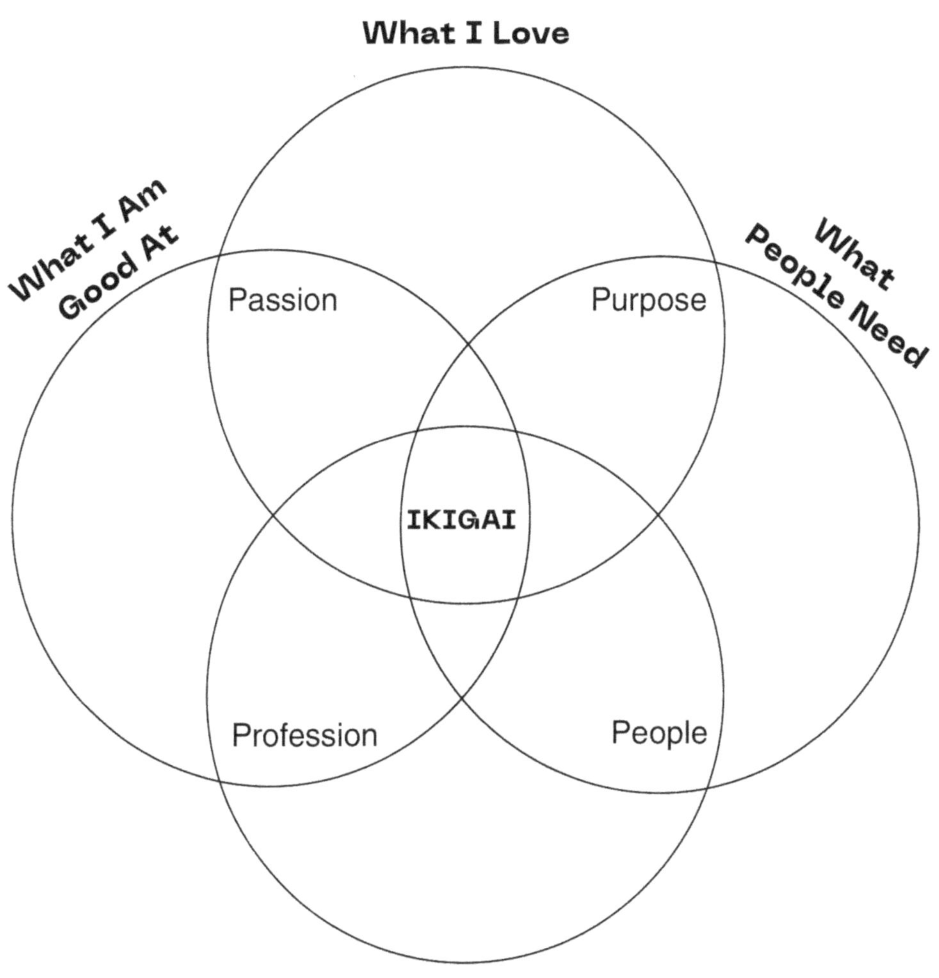


MY PURPOSE STATEMENT

# WHAT IS YOUR IKIGAI?

Complete Your Ikigai Map & Purpose Statement

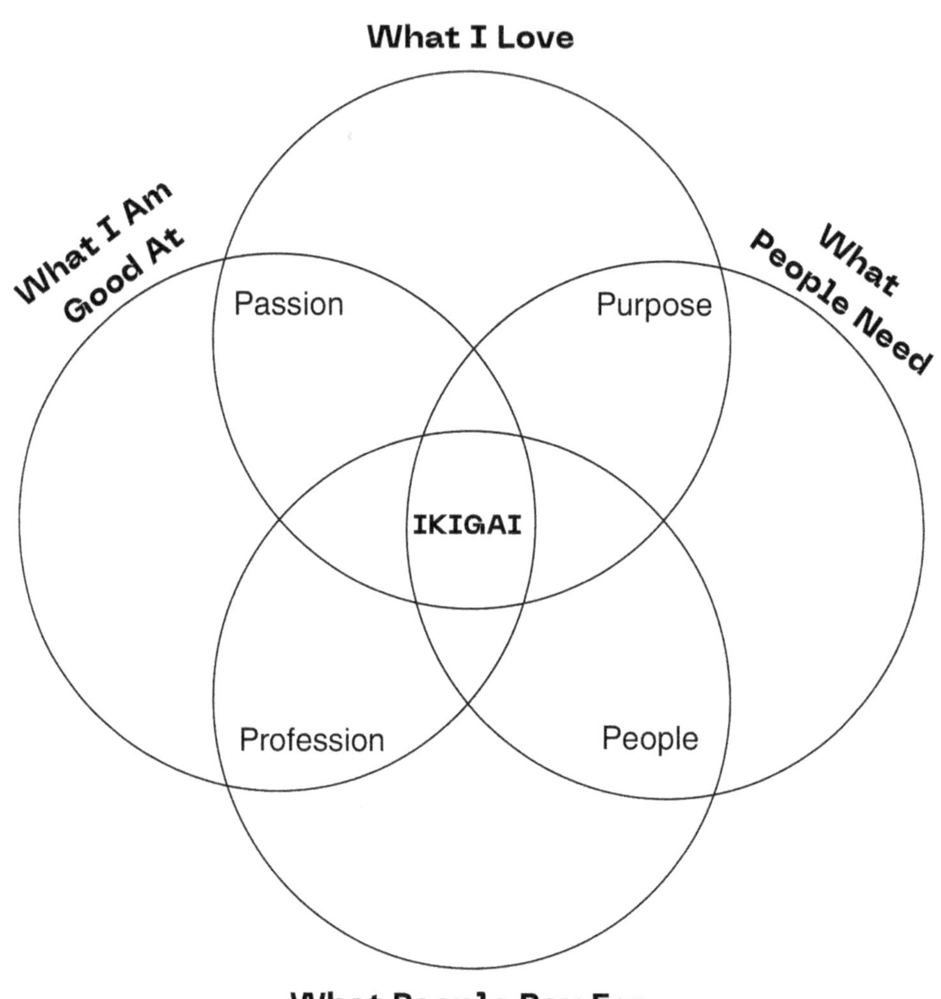


MY PURPOSE STATEMENT

# AFFIRMATIONS

Affirmations serve as powerful tools to boost your confidence, enhance your self-belief, and manifest your dreams into reality. By repeating positive statements, you will rewire your mind to focus on the good, the possible, and the achievable.

Affirmations act as gentle reminders that you are capable, worthy, and deserving of all the wonderful things life has to offer. They create a mindset shift toward optimism and gratitude, guiding you toward a brighter, more fulfilling future. Embrace affirmations as a daily practice to nurture your mind, uplift your spirit, and create a life of abundance.

## Look In The Mirror & Tell Yourself

- ☑ I am a winner. I always win.
- ☑ I am excellent at all times.
- ☑ I am positive, free of negativity.
- ☑ I love myself. I trust myself.
- ☑ I am making my life better.
- ☑ I attract abundant people.
- ☑ I am healthy, wealthy and free.

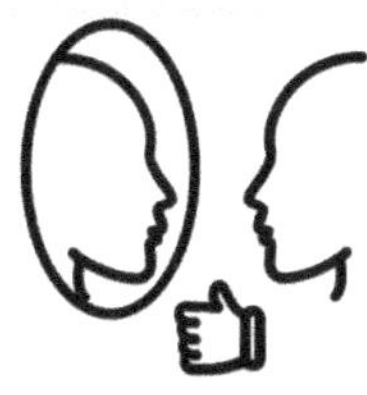

# Daily
## AFFIRMATIONS

- I am confident and comfortable in my own skin

- I'm so grateful for all of the adventures I experience daily

- I have released my attachment to the desires of the ego

- I am the best version of myself

- I welcome opportunities to learn and grow

- I'm so grateful for my healthy and strong body

- I love that my talents bring me money, success, and joy

- I add massive value, therefore I am a lucrative money magnet

- I am surrounded by positive and happy people who support me

- I am co-creating with the universe to uplift the world

- I am beautiful, confident, and loved

- I do what I want, when I want. I am FREE

- I love people. I see oneness everywhere I look

- I know my ikigai, I am living my purpose, and I love my life

- GOD Loves Me and I love everything about myself

- Every day, in every way, I keep getting better and better

- Health, Wealth, Love, and Happiness are Abundant in my life!

- Everything is PERFECT!

# BELIEVE

- GOD loves me abundantly
- I am blessed, protected, and highly favored by GOD
- I love and accept myself completely, forever
- My body is a temple of perfect health and vitality
- I create positive experiences in my life
- I believe in my abilities and strengths
- I forgive myself and others, freeing my spirit
- Love surrounds me at all times
- My thoughts are empowered by positivity & abundance
- I am unstoppable! I am achieving all my goals
- I release fear and step into confident courage
- The universe works in my favor
- I am a magnet for joy and fulfillment
- I deserve abundant love and acceptance
- My focus today is on peace
- I embrace my individuality
- I respect my body
- I eat healthy foods
- I believe in my path
- Abundance comes to me effortlessly
- I release the past and live in the present
- Love comes to me freely, abundantly
- My thoughts are positive and empowering
- Success is mine by birth
- I released all doubt, I am confident
- The universe supports my dreams
- I have excellent character
- I am worthy of kindness and compassion
- Today, I prioritize my needs

# Your Life is a Work of Art

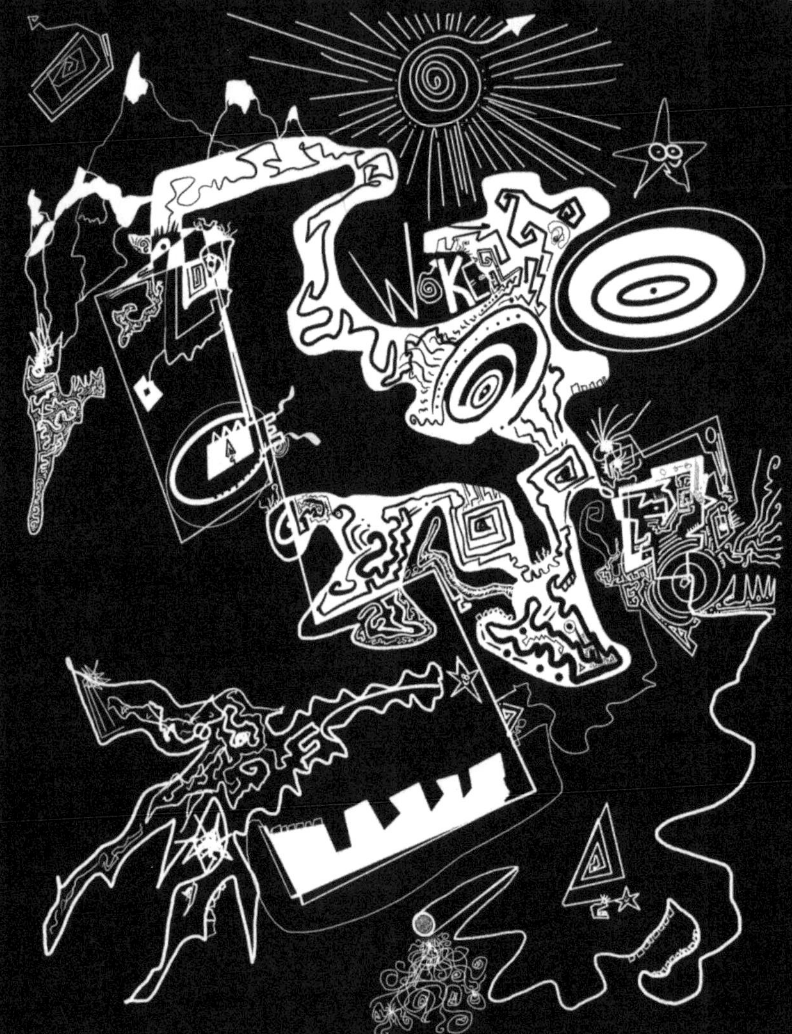


# Enjoy the Process of Creating Your Masterpiece

I added a few extra pages with some of my all-time favorite activities! This is a habit tracker that I like to use to improve my habits on a weekly basis. Try it out for a few weeks and be aware of your transformation. Share results! 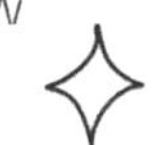

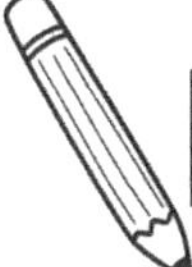

# HABIT TRACKER

## EXAMPLE

| ACTIVITY | M | T | W | T | F | S | S |
|---|---|---|---|---|---|---|---|
| Drink Water with Fresh Lemon | ✓ | ✓ | | | | | |
| Pray + Meditate + Stretch | ✓ | ✓ | | | | | |
| Joyful Journal Writing | ✓ | ✓ | | | | | |
| Healthy Smoothie for Breakfast | ✓ | ✓ | | | | | |
| 33+ Minutes of Exercise | ✓ | ✓ | | | | | |
| Eat a Healthy Lunch | ✓ | ✓ | | | | | |
| Free Time in Nature + Grounding | ✓ | ✓ | | | | | |
| Speak to 3+ New People | ✓ | ✓ | | | | | |
| Read 9+ Pages of a Good Book | ✓ | ✓ | | | | | |

### Weekly Goal

- Exercise 1+ hour daily
- Follow up with art collectors
- Finish the next book manuscript

### What Specific Habits Will You Improve This Week?

I will improve my communication with people. I can reach out and voice my opinions more often.
Get better at following up by setting reminders on my phone calendar to message/call people.

## Week of _2/29/24

More On The Next Page >>>>>>

# HABIT TRACKER

| ACTIVITY | M | T | W | T | F | S | S |
|---|---|---|---|---|---|---|---|

**Weekly Goal**

**What Specific Habits Will You Improve This Week?**

**Week of __/__/__**

68

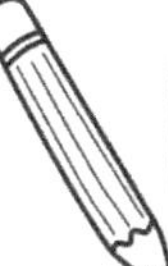# HABIT TRACKER
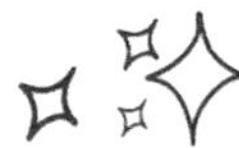

| ACTIVITY | M | T | W | T | F | S | S |
|---|---|---|---|---|---|---|---|

**Weekly Goal**

**What Specific Habits Will You Improve This Week?**

## Week of __ / __ / __

69

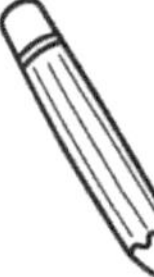

# HABIT TRACKER

| ACTIVITY | M | T | W | T | F | S | S |
| --- | --- | --- | --- | --- | --- | --- | --- |

Weekly Goal

What Specific Habits Will You Improve This Week?

**Week of __ / __ / __**

70

# HABIT TRACKER

| ACTIVITY | M | T | W | T | F | S | S |
|---|---|---|---|---|---|---|---|
| | ○ | ○ | ○ | ○ | ○ | ○ | ○ |
| | ○ | ○ | ○ | ○ | ○ | ○ | ○ |
| | ○ | ○ | ○ | ○ | ○ | ○ | ○ |
| | ○ | ○ | ○ | ○ | ○ | ○ | ○ |
| | ○ | ○ | ○ | ○ | ○ | ○ | ○ |
| | ○ | ○ | ○ | ○ | ○ | ○ | ○ |
| | ○ | ○ | ○ | ○ | ○ | ○ | ○ |
| | ○ | ○ | ○ | ○ | ○ | ○ | ○ |
| | ○ | ○ | ○ | ○ | ○ | ○ | ○ |

**Weekly Goal**

**What Specific Habits Will You Improve This Week?**

**Week of __ / __ / __**

71

# CREATIVE JOURNALING

The next few pages include blank journal pages, graphics, and plenty of space for you to draw some abstract art. Writing and drawing are two of the most therapeutic activities you can do, especially if done in the sun. Use these as you wish and have fun expressing your creativity!

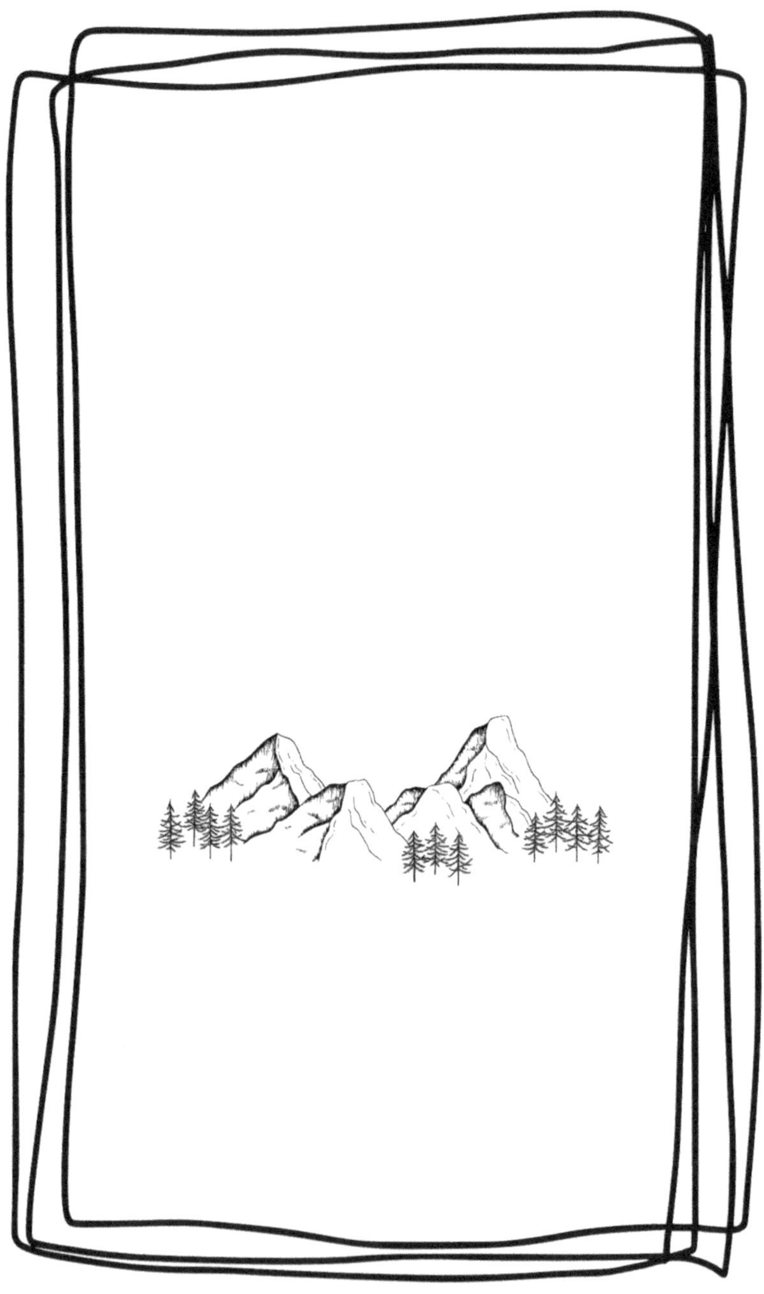

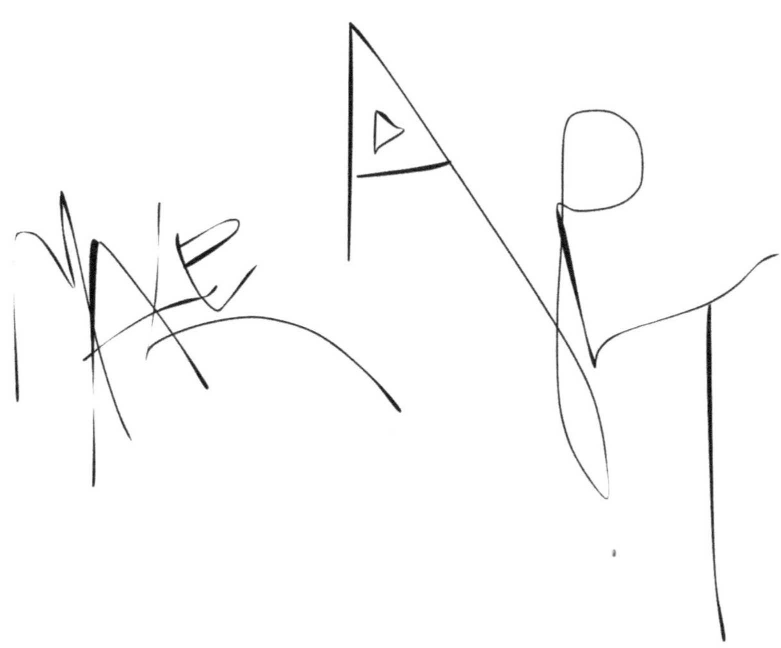
MAKE ART

# Journal

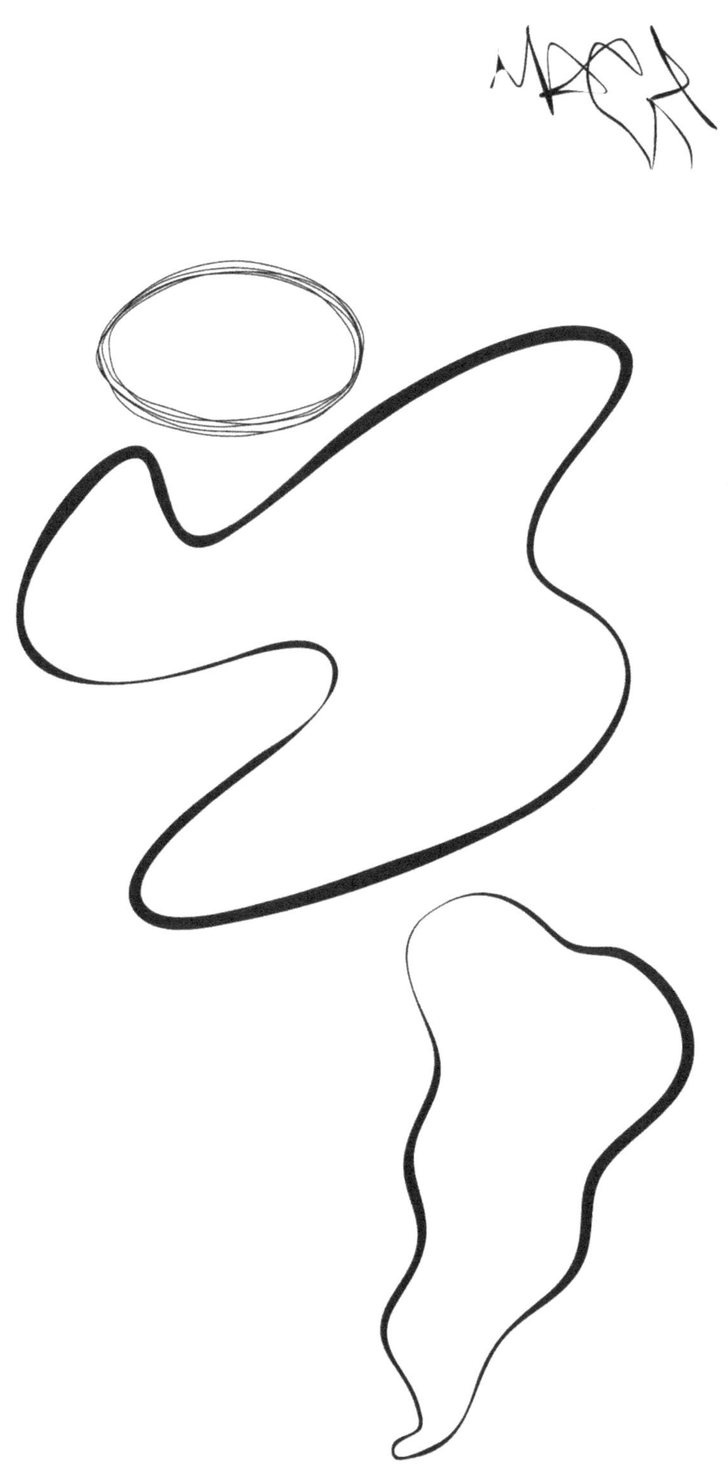

# Journal

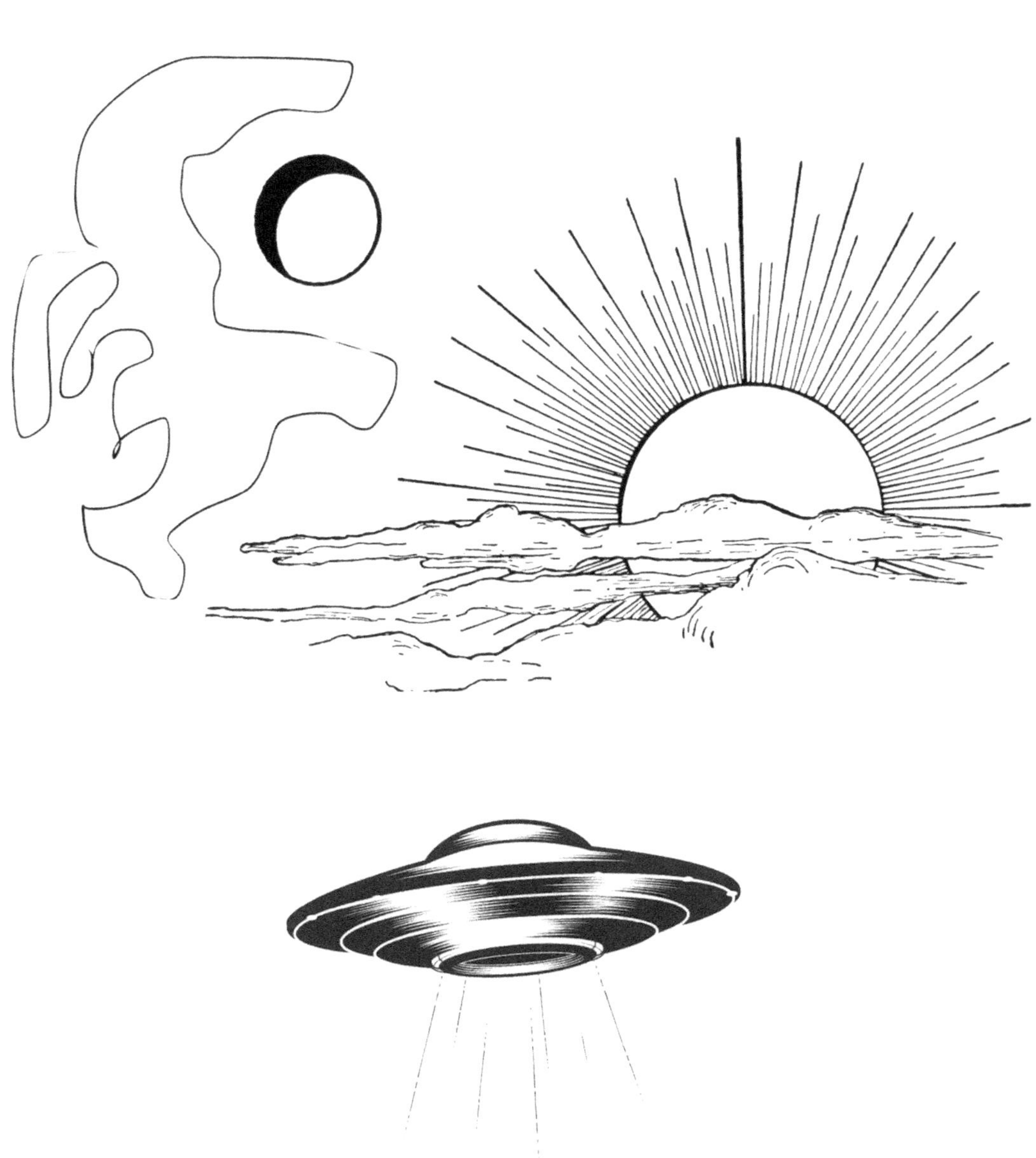

# Journal

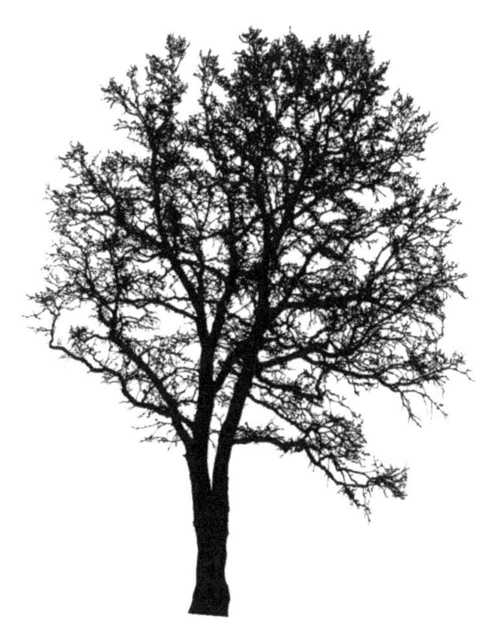

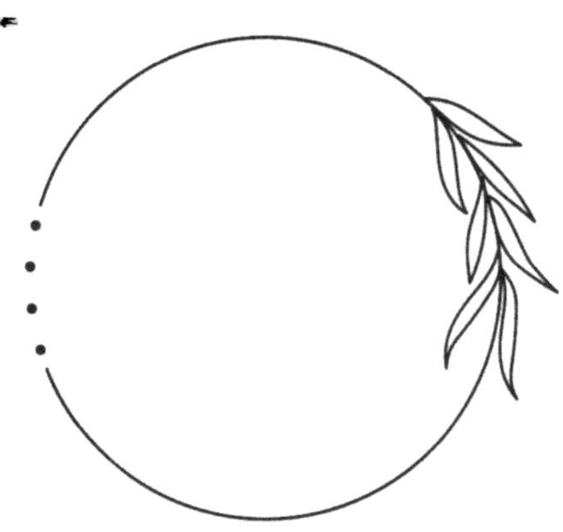

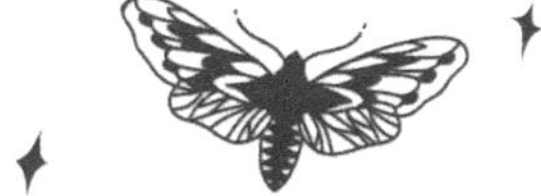

# Journal

DRAW SOMETHIN

# Journal

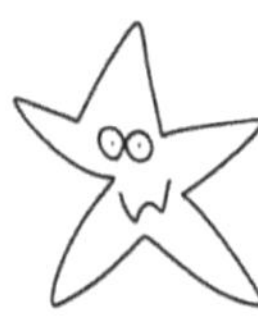

# APPRECIATE YOUR GROWTH

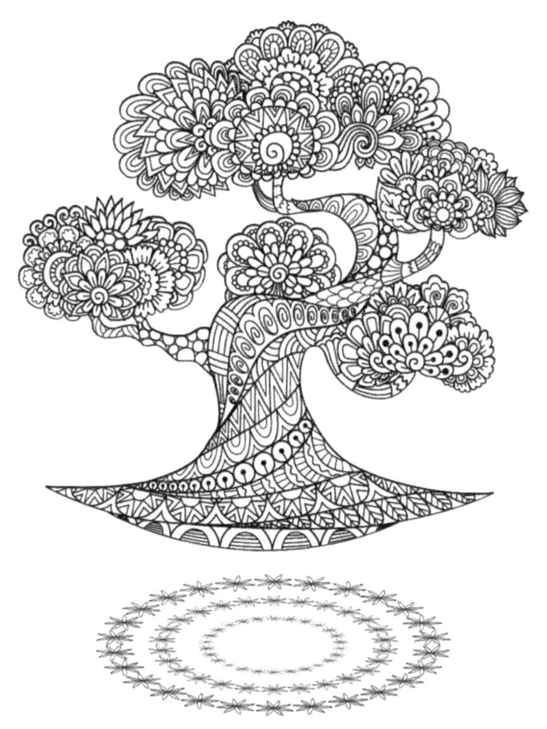

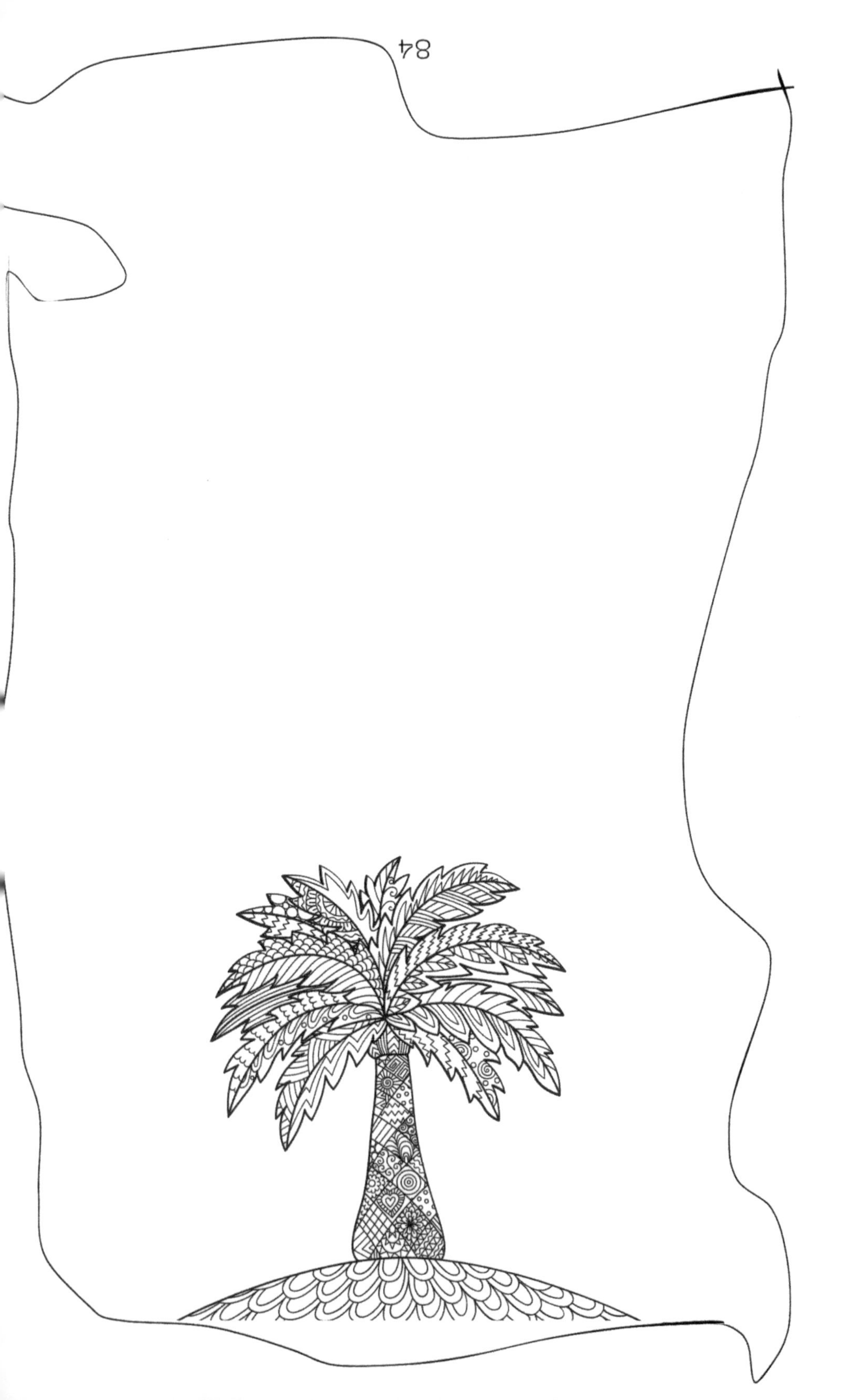

84

# Journal

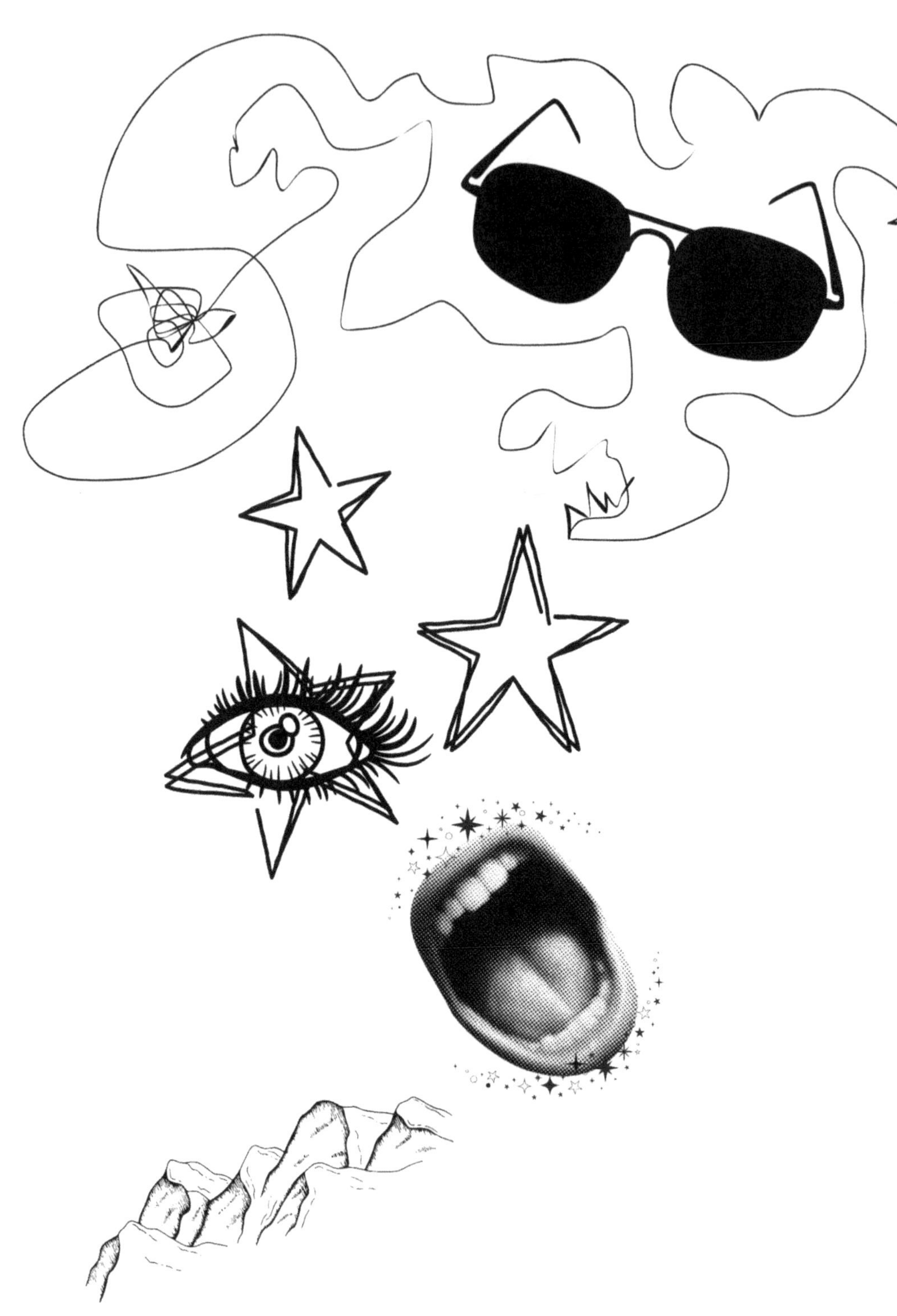

# Journal

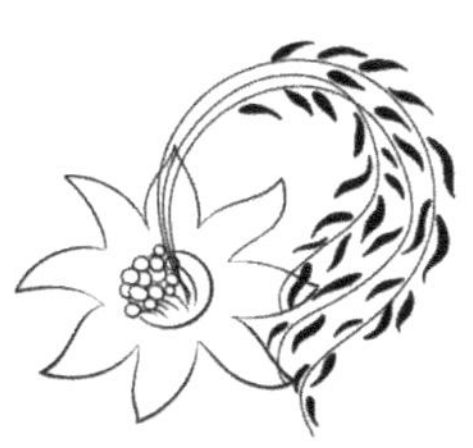

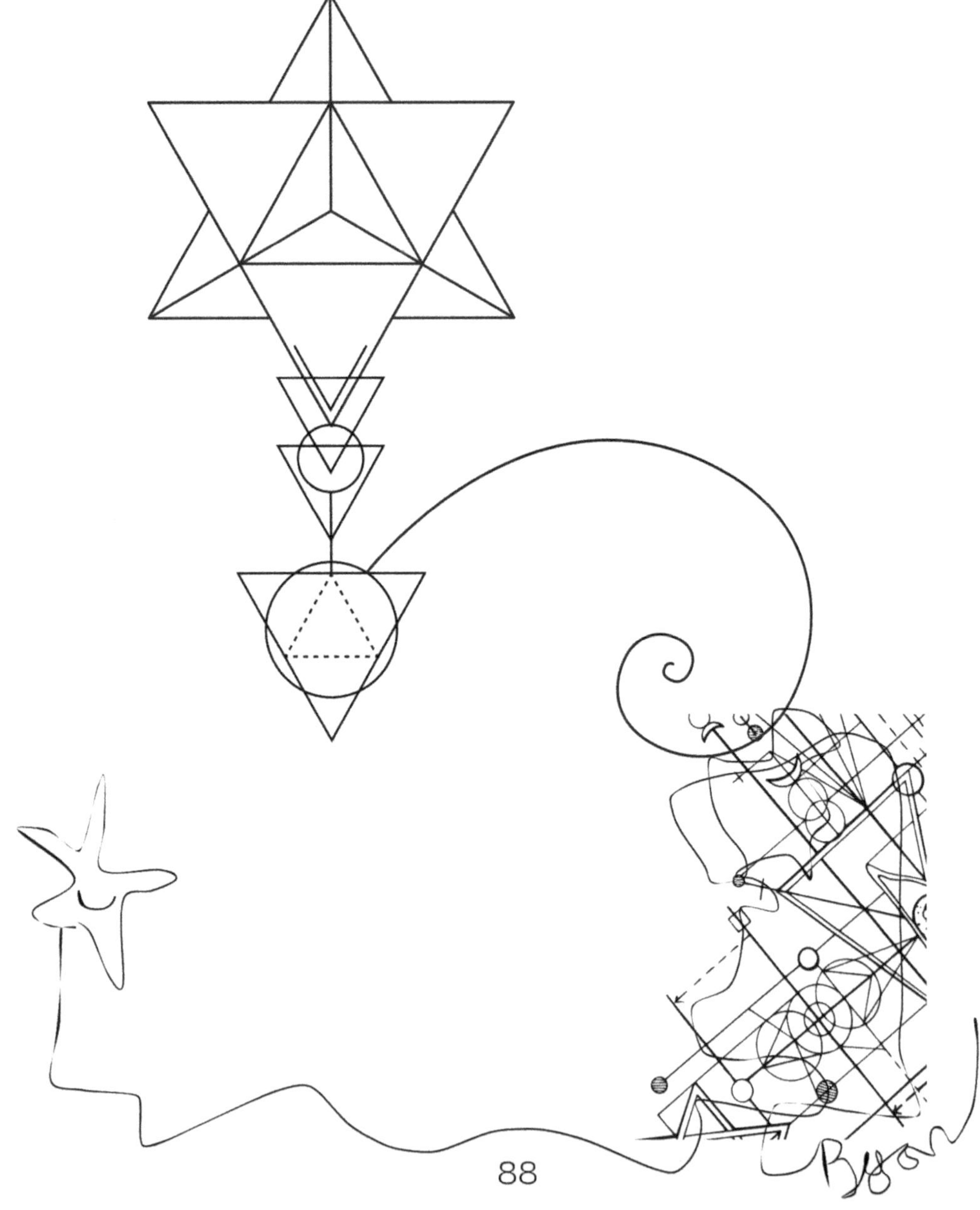

# Journal

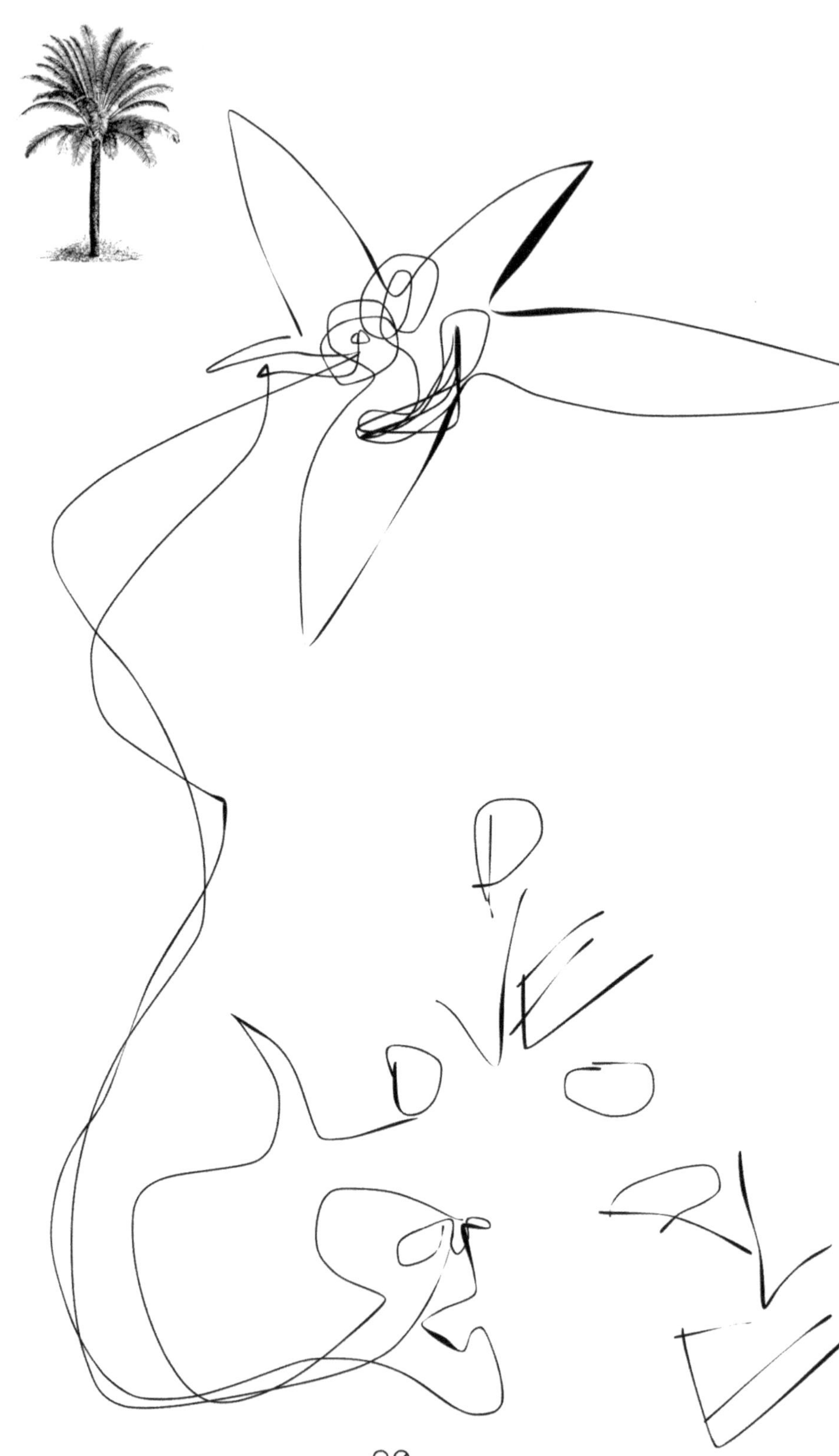

# Journal

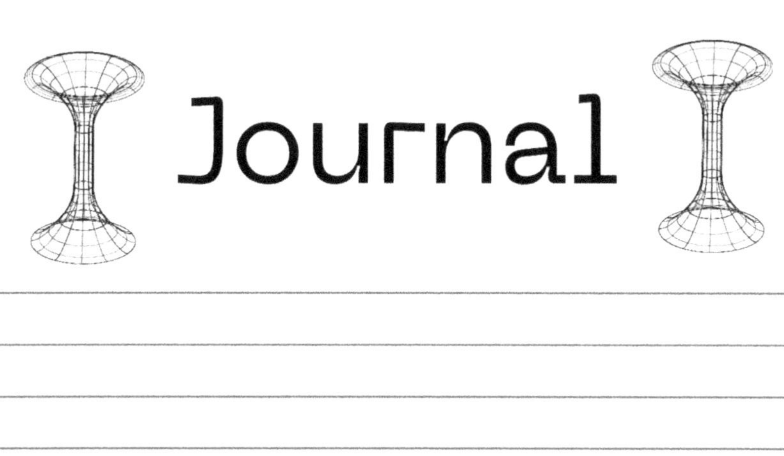

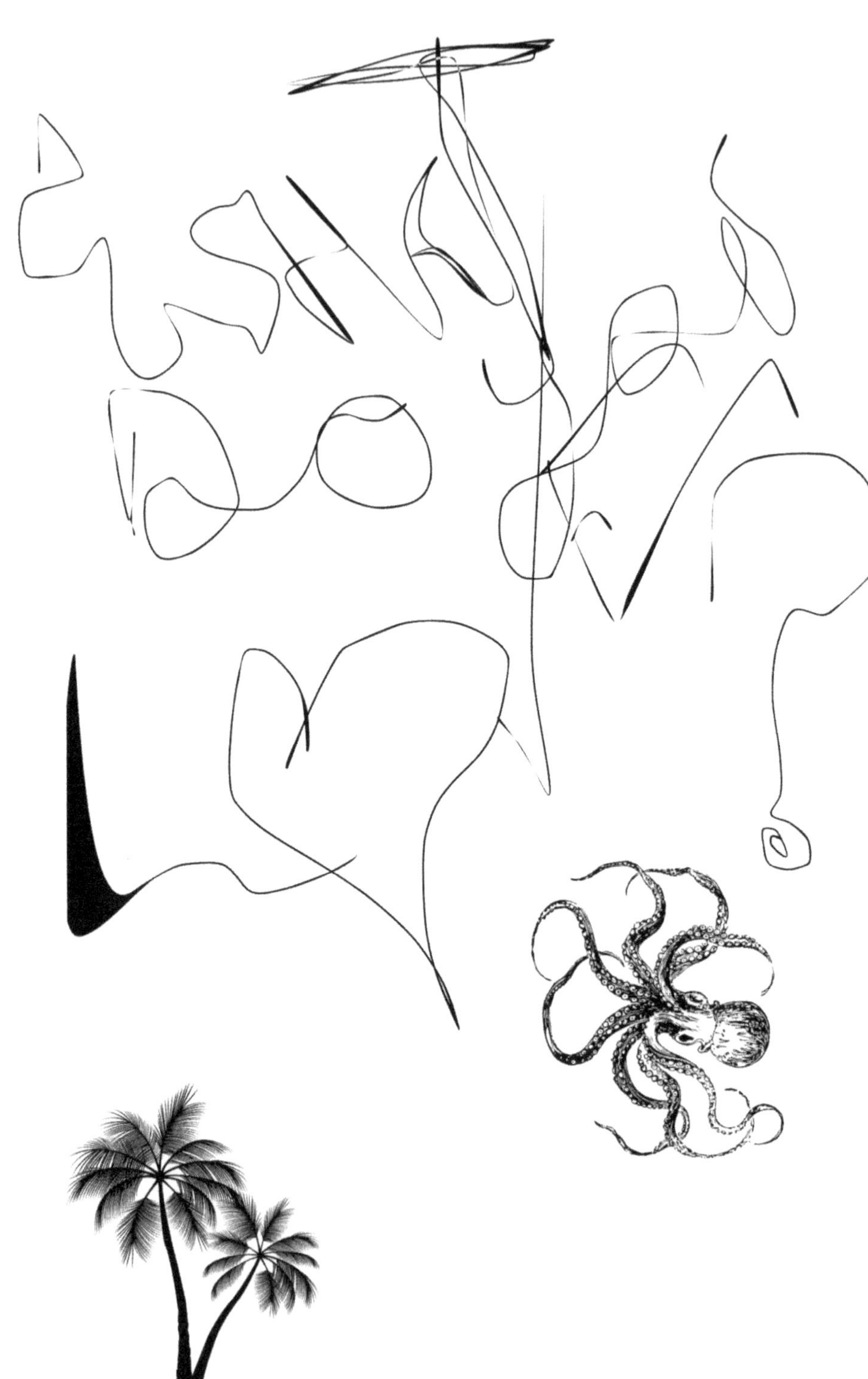

# Journal

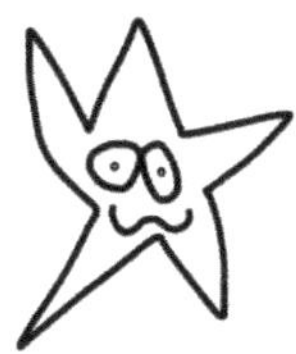

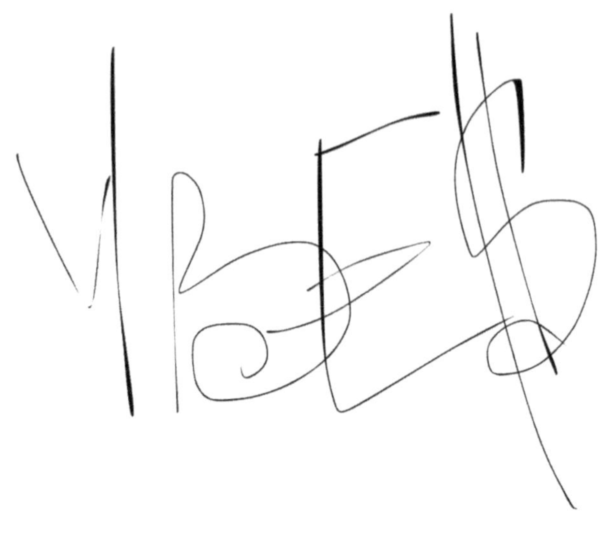

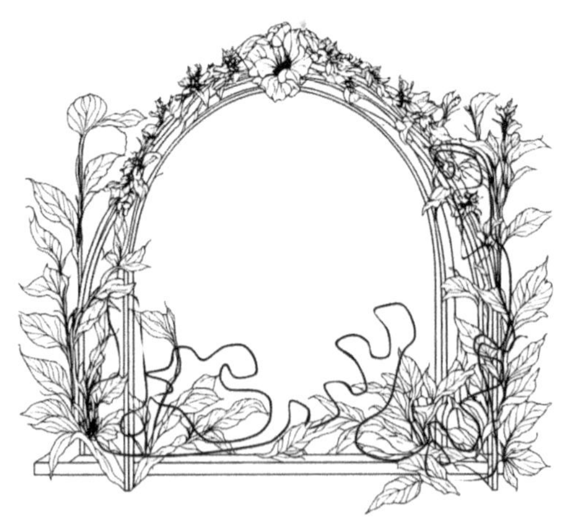

# Journal

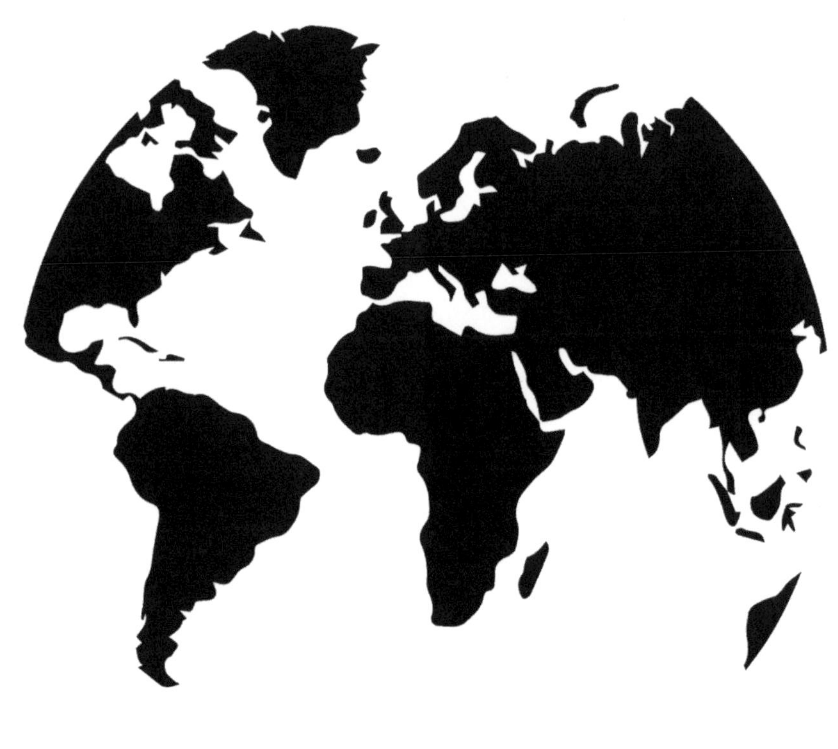
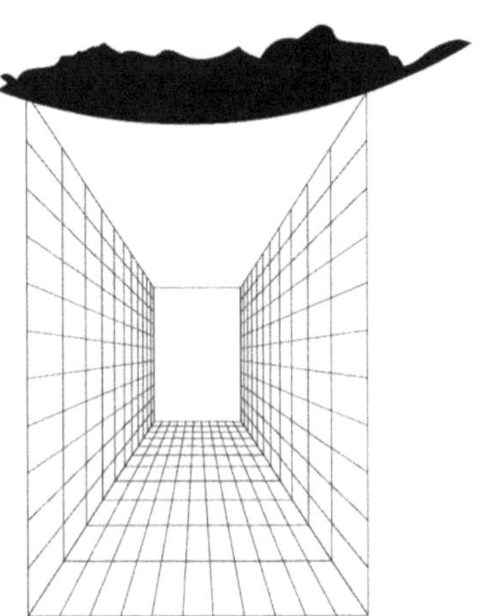

# Journal

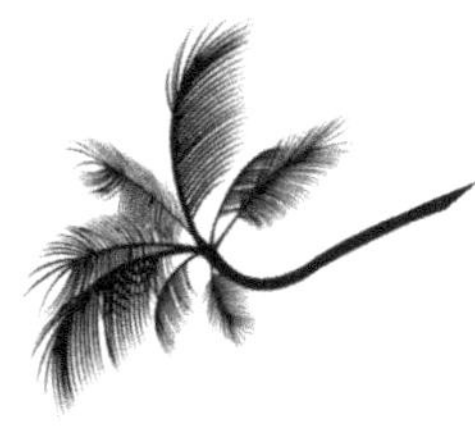

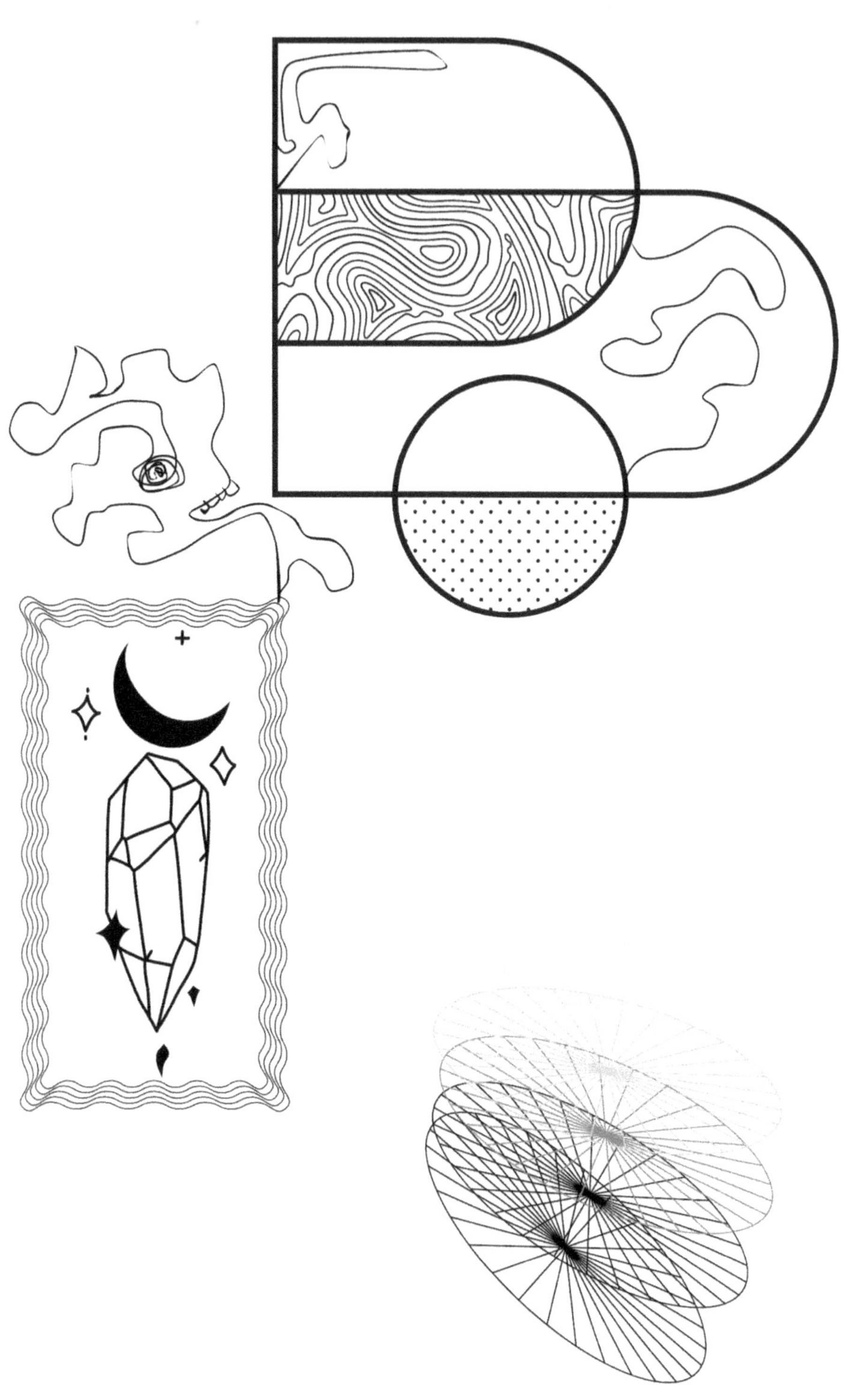

# What Is Your WHY?

Do you have clarity of purpose? Do you know yourself better?
Have you decided the next phase of your Super Star journey?
Write down some key learnings and your favorite takeaways.
Share your success with others as you uplift the world!

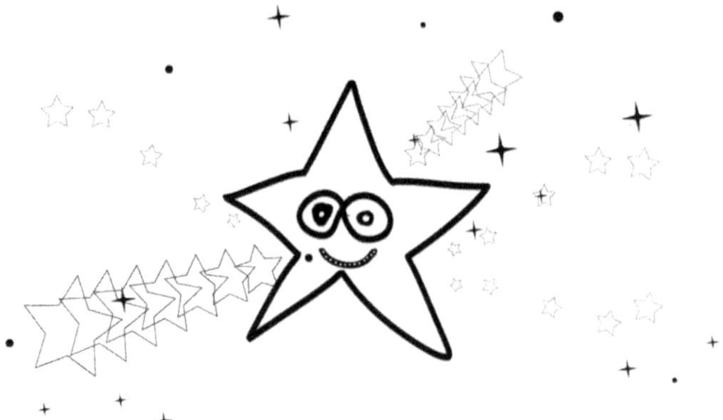

Congratulations! You have discovered your ikigai, you know your WHY, and you have the tools you need to re-program your mind for abundant success.

Everything in this book was written to create clarity, help you organize your life, and shift your paradigm. Use these tools to empower your mind, focus on your purpose, be more accountable, and have more fun!

NOW it's time to fully embody your WHY and create the most abundant life you can imagine. Remain focused, be intentional, and persevere. You can be, do, and have anything you want. Believe it. Do it. Win Abundantly!

Thank you for trusting me with your time and attention. I appreciate your exceptional willingness to learn, as well as your potent ability to accept and create change. Let's go to the next level. I believe in you.

You are a Super Star!


Peace, Love, and Blessings Abundantly,
Bijan Machen

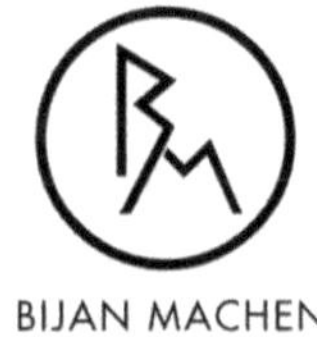

BIJAN MACHEN

If you're interested in learning more
about how you can master your mind and live life
on purpose, check out my other written works
**IKIGUIDE** and **ABUNDANCE ALERT**

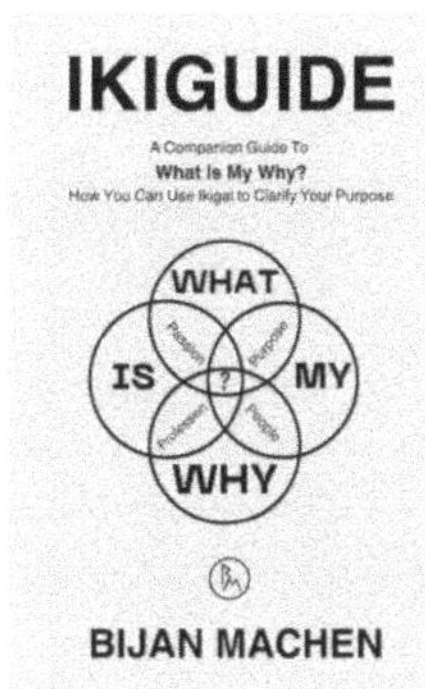
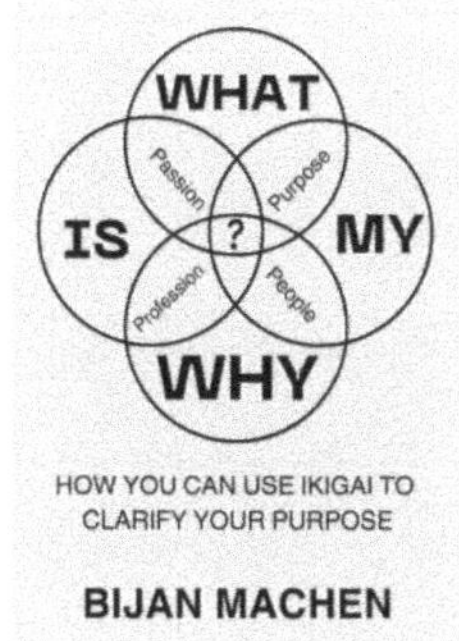
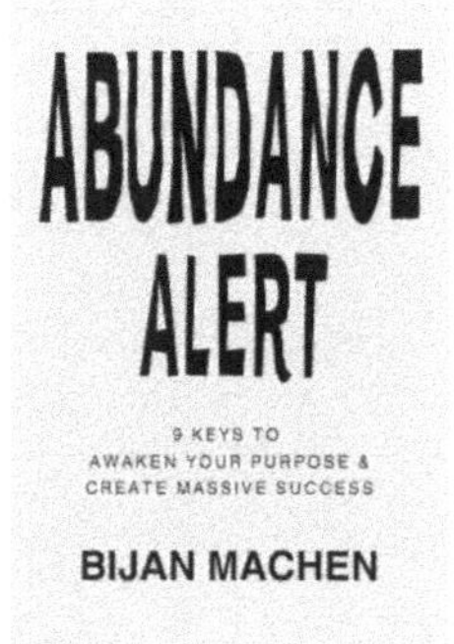

If you enjoyed this experience,
I invite you to leave a review on Amazon.
Thank you!

Spread The Love!
Feel free to share your favorite pages from
the book and tag me on social media.

@bijanmachen
#AbundanceAlert
#WhatIsMyWHY
#IKIGUIDE